S0-BRP-427

THE TIDINGS BROUGHT TO MARY : *A Mystery* : *By*

PAUL CLAUDEL : *Translated from the French by* LOUISE MORGAN SILL

NEW HAVEN, CONNECTICUT
YALE UNIVERSITY PRESS
MDCCCCXVI

Copyright, 1916, by Yale University Press
Printed in the United States of America

———

First published, June, 1916
Second printing, November, 1918
Third printing, November, 1927

30014

CONTENTS

Prologue

The barn at Combernon.   It is a lofty edifice, with square pillars that support a vaulted roof.   It is empty except for the right wing, which is still filled with straw; and straws are scattered about on the floor, which is of well-trampled earth.   At the back is a large double door in the thick wall, with complicated bars and bolts. On the valves of the door are painted rude images of St. Peter and St. Paul, one holding the keys, the other the sword.   The scene is lighted by a large yellow wax candle in an iron socket fastened to one of the pillars.

The scenes of the drama take place at the close of the Middle Ages, seen conventionally, as mediæval poets might have imagined classic antiquity.

The time is night, merging into the hours of dawn.

Enter, on a heavy horse, a man wearing a black cloak, and with a leathern bag on the horse's croup behind him, PIERRE DE CRAON. *His gigantic shadow moves across the wall, the floor, the pillars.*

Suddenly, from behind a pillar, VIOLAINE *steps out to meet him.   She is tall and slender, and her feet are bare.   Her gown is of coarse woollen stuff, and upon her head is a linen coif at once peasant-like and monastic.*

I

VIOLAINE (*laughingly raising her hands toward him, with the forefingers crossed*): Halt, my lord cavalier! Dismount!

PIERRE DE CRAON: Violaine! (*He gets off the horse.*

VIOLAINE: Softly, Master Pierre! Is that the way one leaves the house, like a thief without an honest greeting to the ladies?

PIERRE DE CRAON: Violaine, take yourself off. It is the dead of night, and we are here alone, the two of us.

And you know that I am not such a very safe man.

VIOLAINE: I am not afraid of you, mason! A man is not wicked merely because he wants to be!

And a man doesn't do with me just as he wills!

Poor Pierre! You did not even succeed in killing me

With your wretched knife! Nothing but a little snick on my arm which nobody has seen.

PIERRE DE CRAON: Violaine, you must forgive me.

VIOLAINE: It is for that I came.

PIERRE DE CRAON: You are the first woman I ever laid hands on. The devil, who always seizes his chance, took possession of me.

VIOLAINE: But you found me stronger than him.

PIERRE DE CRAON: Violaine, I am even more dangerous now than I was then.

VIOLAINE: Must we then fight once more?

2

PIERRE DE CRAON: Even my very presence here is baleful. (*Silence*.

VIOLAINE: I don't know what you mean.

PIERRE DE CRAON: Had I not my work? Stones enough to choose and gather, wood enough to join, and metals to melt and mould.

My own work, that suddenly I should lay an impious and lustful hand on the work of another, a living being?

VIOLAINE: In my father's house, the house of your host! Lord! what would they have said if they had known? But I concealed it well.

And they all take you for a sincere and blameless man, just as they did before.

PIERRE DE CRAON: Under appearances, God judges the heart.

VIOLAINE: We three then will guard the secret.

PIERRE DE CRAON: Violaine!

VIOLAINE: Master Pierre?

PIERRE DE CRAON: Stand there near the candle that I may see you well.

(*She stands, smiling, under the candle. He looks a long while at her.*

VIOLAINE: Have you looked at me long enough?

PIERRE DE CRAON: Who are you, young girl, and what part in you has God reserved to himself. That the hand which touches you with fleshly desire should in that same instant be thus

Withered, as if it had approached too near the mystery of his dwelling-place?

VIOLAINE: What has happened to you, then, since last year?

PIERRE DE CRAON: The very next day after that one you remember . . .

VIOLAINE: Well — ?

PIERRE DE CRAON: I discovered in my side the horrible scourge.

VIOLAINE: The scourge, you say? What scourge?

PIERRE DE CRAON: Leprosy, the same we read of in the book of Moses.

VIOLAINE: What is leprosy?

PIERRE DE CRAON: Have you never heard of the woman who lived alone among the rocks of the Géyn.

Veiled from head to foot, and with a rattle in her hand?

VIOLAINE: That malady, Master Pierre?

PIERRE DE CRAON: Such a scourge it is
That he who has it in its most malicious form
Must be set apart at once,
For there is no living man so healthy that leprosy cannot taint him.

VIOLAINE: Why, then, are you still at liberty among us?

PIERRE DE CRAON: The Bishop gave me a dispensation, and you must know how few people I see,

Except my workmen to give them orders, and my
malady is as yet secret and concealed.

And, were I not there, who would give away those
new-born churches whom God has confided to
my care, on their wedding day?

VIOLAINE: Is that why nobody has seen you this
time at Combernon?

PIERRE DE CRAON: I could not avoid returning here,

Because it is my duty to open the side of Monsanvierge

And to unseal the wall for each new flight of
doves that seek entrance into the high Ark
whose gates may only open toward heaven!

And this time we led to the altar an illustrious
victim, a solemn censer,

The Queen herself, mother of the King, ascending
in her own person,

For her son deprived of his kingdom.

And now I return to Rheims.

VIOLAINE: Maker of doors, let me open this one
for you.

PIERRE DE CRAON: Was there no one else at the
farm to do me this service?

VIOLAINE: The servant likes to sleep, and willingly
gave me the keys.

PIERRE DE CRAON: Have you no fear or horror of
the leper?

VIOLAINE: There is God, He knows how to protect me.

PIERRE DE CRAON: Give me the key, then.

VIOLAINE: No. Let me. You do not understand
the working of these old doors.

Indeed! Do you take me for a dainty damsel

Whose taper fingers are used to nothing rougher
than the spur, light as the bone of a bird, that
arms the heel of her new knight?

You shall see!

(*She turns the keys in the two grinding locks
and draws the bolts.*

PIERRE DE CRAON: This iron is very rusty.

VIOLAINE: The door is no longer used. But the
road is shorter this way.

(*She strains at the bar.*

I have opened the door!

PIERRE DE CRAON: What could resist such an
assailant?

What a dust! the old valve from top to bottom
creaks and moves,

The black spiders run away, the old nests crumble,
and the door at last opens from the centre.

(*The door opens; through the darkness can
be seen the meadows and the harvest. A
feeble glimmer in the east.*

VIOLAINE: This little rain has done everybody
good.

PIERRE DE CRAON: The dust in the road will be
well laid.

VIOLAINE (*in a low voice, affectionately*): Peace to
you, Pierre!
> (*Silence. And, suddenly, sonorous and clear
> and very high in the heaven, the first
> tolling of the Angelus. Pierre takes off
> his hat, and both make the sign of the
> cross.*

VIOLAINE (*her hands clasped and her face raised to
heaven, in a voice beautifully clear and touching*):
REGINA CÆLI, LÆTARE, ALLELUIA!
> (*Second tolling.*

PIERRE DE CRAON (*in a hollow voice*): QUIA QUEM
MERUISTI PORTARE, ALLELUIA!
> (*Third tolling.*

VIOLAINE: RESURREXIT SICUT DIXIT, ALLELUIA!

PIERRE DE CRAON: ORA PRO NOBIS DEUM.
> (*Pause.*

VIOLAINE: GAUDE ET LÆTARE, VIRGO MARIA,
ALLELUIA!

PIERRE DE CRAON! QUIA RESURREXIT DOMINUS
VERE, ALLELUIA! (*Peal of the Angelus.*

PIERRE DE CRAON (*very low*): OREMUS. DEUS
QUI PER RESURRECTIONEM FILII TUI DOMINI
NOSTRI JESU CRISTI MUNDUM LÆTIFICARE DIG-
NATUS ES, PRÆSTA, QUÆSUMUS, UT PER EJUS
GENITRICEM VIRGINEM MARIAM PERPETUÆ
CAPIAMUS GAUDIA VITÆ. PER EUNDEM DOMI-
NUM NOSTRUM JESUM CHRISTUM QUI TECUM

VIVIT ET REGNAT IN UNITATE SPIRITUS SANCTI DEUS PER OMNIA SÆCULA SÆCULORUM.

VIOLAINE: Amen. *(Both cross themselves.*

PIERRE DE CRAON: How early the Angelus rings!

VIOLAINE: They say matins up there at midnight like the Carthusians.

PIERRE DE CRAON: I shall be at Rheims this evening.

VIOLAINE: Know you well the road?

First along this hedge,

And then by that low house in the grove of elder bushes, under which you will see five or six beehives.

And a hundred paces further on you reach the King's Highway. *(A pause.*

PIERRE DE CRAON: PAX TIBI.

How all creation seems to rest with God in a profound mystery!

That which was hidden grows visible again with Him, and I feel on my face a breath as fresh as roses.

Praise thy God, blessed earth, in tears and darkness!

The fruit is for man, but the flower is for God and the sweet fragrance of all things born.

Thus the virtue of the holy soul that is hidden is subtly revealed, as the mint leaf by its odour.

Violaine, who have opened the door for me, farewell!

I shall never return again to you.

O young tree of the knowledge of Good and Evil,
behold how my dissolution begins because I
have laid my hands upon you,

And already my soul and body are being divided,
as the wine in the vat from the crushed grape!

What matters it? I had no need of woman.

I have never possessed a corruptible woman.

The man who in his heart has preferred God, sees
when he dies his guardian Angel.

The time will soon come when another door opens,

When he who in this life has pleased but few,
having finished his work, falls asleep in the
arms of the eternal Bird:

When through translucent walls looms on all
sides the sombre Paradise,

And the censers of the night mingle their scent with
the odour of the noisome wick as it sputters out.

VIOLAINE: Pierre de Craon, I know that you do
not expect to hear from me any false sighs,
"Poor fellows!" or "Poor Pierres."

Because to him who suffers the consolation of a
joyous comforter is not of much worth, for his
anguish is not to us what it is to him.

Suffer with our Lord.

But know that your evil act is forgotten

So far as it concerns me, and that I am at peace
with you,

And that I do not scorn or abhor you because
you are stricken with the pest and malady,
But I shall treat you like a healthy man, and like
Pierre de Craon, our old friend, whom I respect
and love and fear.
What I say to you is true.

PIERRE DE CRAON: Thank you, Violaine.

VIOLAINE: And now I have something to ask you.

PIERRE DE CRAON: Speak.

VIOLAINE: What is this beautiful story that my father
has told us? What is this "Justice" that you
are building at Rheims, and that will be more
beautiful than Saint-Rémy and Notre-Dame?

PIERRE DE CRAON: It is the church which the guilds
of Rheims gave me to build on the site of the
old Parc-aux-Ouilles,[1]

There where the old Marc-de-l'Evêque[2] was
burned down yesteryear.

Firstly, as a thank-offering to God for seven fat
summers while distress reigned everywhere else
in the kingdom,

For abundant grain and fruit, for cheap and
beautiful wool,

For cloth and parchment profitably sold to the
merchants of Paris and Germany.

Secondly, for the liberties acquired, the privileges
conferred by our Lord the King,

---

[1] Sheep-fold.　　　　[2] The bishop's still.

The old order issued against us by Bishops
  Felix II and Abondant de Cramail
Rescinded by the Pope,
And all that by the aid of the bright sword and
  Champenois coins.
For such is the Christian commonwealth, without
  servile fear,
But that each should have his right, according
  to justice, in marvellous diversity,
That charity may be fulfilled.

VIOLAINE: But of which King and of which Pope
  do you speak? For there are two, and one does
  not know which is the good one.

PIERRE DE CRAON: The good one is he who is
  good to us.

VIOLAINE: You do not speak rightly.

PIERRE DE CRAON: Forgive me. I am only an ig-
  norant man.

VIOLAINE: And whence comes this name given to
  the new parish?

PIERRE DE CRAON: Have you never heard of Saint
  Justice who was martyred in an anise field in
  the time of the Emperor Julian?

(The anise seeds which they put in our ginger-
  bread at the Easter fair.)

As we were trying to divert the waters of a sub-
  terranean spring, to make way for our foundations,

11

We discovered her tomb, with this inscription on
a slab of stone, broken in two: JUSTITIA ANCILLA
DOMINI IN PACE.

The fragile little skull was broken like a nut —
she was a child of eight years —

And a few milk teeth still adhere to the jaw.

For which all Rheims is filled with admiration,
and many signs and miracles follow the body

Which we have laid in a chapel, to await the
completion of our work.

But under the great foundation stone we have
left, like seed, the little teeth.

VIOLAINE: What a beautiful story! And father
also told us that all the ladies of Rheims give
their jewels for the building of the Justice.

PIERRE DE CRAON: We have a great heap of them,
and many Jews around them like flies.

(VIOLAINE *has been looking down and turning
hesitatingly a massive gold ring which she
wears on her fourth finger.*

PIERRE DE CRAON: What ring is that, Violaine?

VIOLAINE: A ring that Jacques gave me.

(*Silence.*

PIERRE DE CRAON: I congratulate you.

(*She holds out the ring to him.*

VIOLAINE: It is not yet settled. My father has said
nothing.

Well! That is what I wanted to tell you.

Take my beautiful ring, which is all I have, and
Jacques gave it to me secretly.

PIERRE DE CRAON: But I do not want it!

VIOLAINE: Take it quickly, or I shall no longer
have the strength to part with it.

(*He takes the ring.*

PIERRE DE CRAON: What will your betrothed say?

VIOLAINE: He is not really my betrothed yet.
The loss of a ring does not change the heart. He
knows me. He will give me another of silver.
This one was too fine for me.

PIERRE DE CRAON (*examining it*): It is of vegetable
gold which, in former times, they knew how to
make with an alloy of honey.

It is as supple as wax, and nothing can break it.

VIOLAINE: Jacques turned it up in the ground when
he was ploughing, in a place where they sometimes find old swords turned quite green, and
pretty bits of glass.

I was afraid to wear such a pagan thing, which
belongs to the dead.

PIERRE DE CRAON: I accept this pure gold.

VIOLAINE: And kiss my sister Justice for me.

PIERRE DE CRAON (*looking suddenly at her, as if struck
with an idea*): Is that all you have to give me
for her? a bit of gold taken off your finger?

VIOLAINE: Will that not be enough to pay for
one little stone?

PIERRE DE CRAON: But Justice is a large stone herself.

VIOLAINE (*laughing*): I am not from the same quarry.

PIERRE DE CRAON: The stone needed for the base is not the stone needed for the pinnacle.

VIOLAINE: Then, if I am a stone, may it be that useful one that grinds the corn, coupled to the twin millstone.

PIERRE DE CRAON: And Justitia also was only a humble little girl at her mother's side.

Until the moment God called her to the confession of faith.

VIOLAINE: But nobody wishes me ill! Is it necessary that I should go preach the Gospel to the Saracens?

PIERRE DE CRAON: It is not for the stone to choose its own place, but for the Master of the Work who chose the stone.

VIOLAINE: Then praised be God who has given me mine now, and I have no longer to seek it. And I ask him for no other.

I am Violaine, I am eighteen years old, my father's name is Anne Vercors, my mother's name is Elisabeth,

My sister's name is Mara, my betrothed is named Jacques. There, that is all, there is nothing more to know.

Everything is perfectly clear, all is arranged
beforehand, and I am very glad.

I am free, I have nothing to trouble me; another
will lead me, the poor man, and he knows everything that there is to do.

Sower of steeples, come to Combernon! we will
give you stone and wood, but you shall not
have the daughter of the house!

And, besides, is this not already the house of God,
the land of God, the service of God?

Have we not charge over lonely Monsanvierge,
which we must feed and guard, providing it
with bread, wine, and wax,

Being a dependency of this lonely eyrie of angels
with half-spread wings?

Thus, as the great lords have their dovecot, we
too have ours, which is known from a great
distance away.

PIERRE DE CRAON: One day as I went through the
forest of Fisme, I heard two beautiful oak trees
talking together,

Praising God for making them immovable on the
spot where they were born.

Now one of them, in the prow of an ocean raft,
makes war upon the Turks,

The other, felled under my care, supports Jehanne,
the good bell in the tower of Laon, whose
voice is heard ten leagues away.

Young girl, in my craft one does not keep one's
eyes in one's pocket.

I know the good stone under the juniper trees,
and the good wood like a master woodpecker;

In the same way, men and women.

VIOLAINE: But not girls, Master Pierre! That
is too subtle for you. And in the first place,
there is nothing at all to know.

PIERRE DE CRAON (*in a low voice*): You love him
dearly, Violaine?

VIOLAINE (*lowering her eyes*): That is a great mystery
between us two.

PIERRE DE CRAON: Blessed be thou in thy pure heart!

Holiness is not to get oneself stoned by the Turks,
or to kiss a leper on the mouth,

But to obey promptly God's commands.

Whether it be

To stay where we are, or to ascend higher.

VIOLAINE: Ah, how beautiful the world is, and how
happy I am!

PIERRE DE CRAON (*speaking low*): Ah, how beautiful
the world is, and how unhappy I am!

VIOLAINE (*pointing to the sky*): Man of the city,
listen! (*Pause.*

Do you hear high up there that little soul singing?

PIERRE DE CRAON: It is the lark!

VIOLAINE: It is the lark, alleluia! The lark of the
Christian earth, alleluia, alleluia!

16

Do you hear it cry four times, he! he! he! he!
higher, higher!

Do you see it, the eager little cross, with its
wings spread, like the seraphim who have
only wings and no feet, singing shrilly before
the throne of God?

PIERRE DE CRAON: I hear it.

And it is thus I heard it once at dawn, on the day
we dedicated my daughter Notre-Dame de la
Couture,

And a golden point gleamed at the topmost pinnacle of this great thing I had made, like a
star new-born!

VIOLAINE: Pierre de Craon, if you had done with
me as you would,

Would you be more happy now because of that,
or I more beautiful?

PIERRE DE CRAON: No, Violaine.

VIOLAINE: And would I still be the same Violaine
whom you loved?

PIERRE DE CRAON: No, not she, but another.

VIOLAINE: And which is better, Pierre,

That I share my joy with you, or that I share your
pain?

PIERRE DE CRAON: Sing far up in the highest
heaven, lark of France!

VIOLAINE: Forgive me, for I am too happy, because
he whom I love

Loves me, and I am sure of him, and I know he loves me, and all is equal between us.

And because God made me to be happy and not for evil nor any sorrow.

PIERRE DE CRAON: Mount to heaven in a single flight! As for me, to ascend a little I must have the whole of a cathedral, with its deep foundations.

VIOLAINE: And tell me that you forgive Jacques for marrying me.

PIERRE DE CRAON: No, I do not forgive him.

VIOLAINE: Hatred does you no good, Pierre, and makes me grieve.

PIERRE DE CRAON: It is you who make me speak. Why do you force me to show the ugly wound that no one sees?

Let me go, and ask me nothing more. We shall not see each other any more.

All the same, I carry away his ring!

VIOLAINE: Leave your hatred in its place, and I will give it back to you when you have need of it.

PIERRE DE CRAON: But besides, Violaine, I am very wretched.

It is hard to be a leper, to bear this shameful wound, knowing that there is no cure and that there is no help for it,

But that each day it spreads and bites deeper; and to be alone, and to suffer one's own poison, to feel oneself alive in corruption,

Not only to taste death once, aye, ten times, but
to miss nothing, even to the end, of the horrible
alchemy of the tomb!

It is you who have brought this evil upon me by
your beauty, for before I saw you I was pure
and happy,

My heart lost in my work and ideas, under another's command.

And now that I command in my turn, and draw
the plans,

Behold, you turn your face toward me with that
poisonous smile.

VIOLAINE: The poison was not in me, Pierre!

PIERRE DE CRAON: I know it, it was in me, and it
is still there, and this sick flesh has not cured
the tainted soul!

O little soul, was it possible that I should see you
and not love you?

VIOLAINE: And certainly you have shown that you
loved me.

PIERRE DE CRAON: It is my fault if the fruit hangs
on the branch?

And who is he who loves and does not desire all?

VIOLAINE: And that is why you tried to destroy
me?

PIERRE DE CRAON: Man, cruelly injured, has his
infernal shades, too, like woman.

VIOLAINE: In what have I failed you?

19

PIERRE DE CRAON: O image of eternal Beauty, thou art not for me!

VIOLAINE: I am not an image!
That is not the way to speak!

PIERRE DE CRAON: Another takes from you that which was for me.

VIOLAINE: The image remains.

PIERRE DE CRAON: Another takes Violaine from me, and leaves me this tainted flesh and this consumed mind.

VIOLAINE: Be a man, Pierre! Be worthy of the flame which consumes you!
And if one must be consumed, let it be like the Paschal-candle, flaming on its golden candelabrum in the midst of the choir for the glory of all the Church!

PIERRE DE CRAON: So many sublime pinnacles! But shall I never see the roof of my own little house under the trees?
So many belfries whose circling shadows write the hour for all the city! But shall I never design an oven, and the room for the children?

VIOLAINE: It was not for me to take for myself alone what belongs to all.

PIERRE DE CRAON: When will the wedding be, Violaine?

VIOLAINE: At Michaelmas, I suppose, when the harvest is done.

PIERRE DE CRAON: On that day, when the bells of Monsanvierge have spoken and are silent, listen well and you will hear me answer them far away at Rheims.

VIOLAINE: Who takes care of you there?

PIERRE DE CRAON: I have always lived like a workman; it is enough for me if I have a bunch of straw between two stones, a leathern coat, and a little bacon on my bread.

VIOLAINE: Poor Pierre!

PIERRE DE CRAON: I am not to be pitied for that; we are set apart.

I do not live as other men, as I am always under the ground with the foundations, or in the sky with the belfry.

VIOLAINE: Well! We could never have lived together! My head swims if I only go up to the hayloft.

PIERRE DE CRAON: This church alone will be my wife, drawn from my side like an Eve of stone, in the slumber of pain.

May I soon feel my great structure rising under me, and lay my hand on this indestructible thing I have made, whose parts hold firmly together, this solid work which I have constructed of strong stone that the Holy Sacrament may be placed there, my work that God inhabits!

I shall never come down again! It is I at whom
they point, that group of young girls with arms
interlaced, on the chequered pavement a hundred feet below!

VIOLAINE: You must come down. Who knows
but I shall have need of you some day?

PIERRE DE CRAON: Farewell, Violaine, my soul, I
shall never see you again!

VIOLAINE: Who knows that you will never see
me again?

PIERRE DE CRAON: Farewell, Violaine!

How many things I have already done! How
many things remain for me to do, how much
building up of habitations!

Darkness, with God.

Not the hours of the office in a breviary, but
the real hours of a cathedral, where the sun
brings light and shade successfully to every
part.

I take away your ring,

And of its little circle I will make golden
seed!

"God caused the deluge to cease," as says the
baptismal psalm,

And I, between the walls of the Justice, shall
imprison the gold of the dawn!

The light of day changes, but not that which I
shall distil under those arches,

Like the light of the human soul, that the Host may dwell in the midst of it.

The soul of Violaine, my child, in whom my heart delights.

There are churches like pits, and others which are like furnaces,

And others so delicately put together, adjusted with such art, that they seem as if they would ring like a bell under a finger-tap.

But that which I am going to build will lie under its own shadow like condensed gold, and like a pyx full of manna!

VIOLAINE: O Master Pierre, what a beautiful stained-glass window you gave to the monks of Clinchy!

PIERRE DE CRAON: The staining of glass is not my art, though I know something of it.

But, before the glass is made, the architect, by his knowledge of arrangement, makes the stone framework like a filter in the waves of God's Light,

And gives to the whole edifice its individual lustre, as to a pearl.

(MARA VERCORS *enters and watches them without being seen.*

And now farewell! The sun is risen, and I ought already to be far on my road.

VIOLAINE: Farewell, Pierre!

PIERRE DE CRAON: Farewell, Violaine!

VIOLAINE: Poor Pierre!

> (*She looks at him with eyes full of tears,
> hesitates, and offers him her hand. He
> seizes it, and while he holds it between his
> own she leans towards him and kisses him
> on the face.*
>
> MARA *makes a gesture of surprise and goes
> out.*
>
> PIERRE DE CRAON *and* VIOLAINE *go out by
> the different doors.*

Act One: Scene One

The kitchen of Combernon, a spacious room having a great fireplace with an emblazoned mantel; in the middle of the room a long table and all the domestic utensils, as in a picture by Breughel. THE MOTHER, *stooping before the hearth, tries to revive the fire.* ANNE VERCORS, *standing, looks at her. He is a tall and strong man of sixty years, with a full blond beard streaked with much white.*

THE MOTHER (*without turning round*): Why do you look at me like that?

ANNE VERCORS (*thinking*): The end, already! It is like coming to the last page in a picture book. "When the night had passed, the woman having revived the household fire . . .," and the humble and touching story is finished.

It is as if I were no longer here. There she is, before my eyes, yet seeming already like something only remembered.   (*Aloud.*

O wife it is a month since we were married
With a ring which is shaped like *Oui*,
A month of which each day is a year.
And for a long time you were fruitless
Like a tree which gives nothing but shade.

25

And one day we looked at each other
And it was the middle of our life,
Elisabeth! and I saw the first wrinkles on thy
forehead and around thine eyes.
And, as on our wedding day,
We clasped and embraced each other, no longer
with lightness of heart,
But with the tenderness and compassion and
piety of our mutual trust.
And between us was our child and the modesty
Of this sweet narcissus, Violaine.
And then the second was born to us,
Mara the black. Another daughter, and not a
son. (*Pause.*
Well now, say what you have to say, for I know
When you begin speaking without looking at you,
saying something and nothing. Come now!
THE MOTHER: You know well that one can tell you
nothing. You are never there, and I must even
catch you to sew on a button.
And you do not listen to one, but like a watch-
dog you watch,
Only attentive to the noises of the door.
But men never understand anything.
ANNE VERCORS: Now the little girls are grown up.
THE MOTHER: They? No.
ANNE VERCORS: To whom are we going to marry
them all?

THE MOTHER: Marry them, Anne, say you?
We have plenty of time to think of that.

ANNE VERCORS: Oh, deceit of woman! Tell me!
When think you anything
But first you do not say just the contrary; maliciousness! I know thee.

THE MOTHER: I won't say anything more.

ANNE VERCORS: Jacques Hury.

THE MOTHER: Well?

ANNE VERCORS: There. I will give him Violaine . . .
And he will take the place of the son I have not
had. He is an upright and industrious man.
I have known him since he was a little lad, and
his mother gave him to us. It is I who have
taught him everything,
Grain, cattle, servants, arms, tools, our neighbours,
our betters, custom — God —
The weather, the nature of this ancient soil,
How to reflect before speaking.
I have seen him develop into a man while he was
looking at me and the beard grow around his
kind face,
As he is now, straight-backed and tight like the
ears of the barley.
And he was never one of those who contradict,
but who reflect, like the earth which receives
all kinds of grain.
And that which is false, not taking root, dies;

And so, one may not say that he believes in truth,
but rather that it grows within him, having
found nourishment.

THE MOTHER: How do you know, if they love each
other or not?

ANNE VERCORS: Violaine

Will do what I tell her.

As for him, I know that he loves her, and you
too know it.

Yet the blockhead dares not speak to me. But
I will give her to him if he wants her. So shall
it be.

THE MOTHER: Yes.

No doubt that is as it should be.

ANNE VERCORS: Have you nothing more to say?

THE MOTHER: What, then?

ANNE VERCORS: Very well, I will go seek him.

THE MOTHER: What, seek him? Anne!

ANNE VERCORS: I want everything to be settled
at once. I will tell you why presently.

THE MOTHER: What have you to tell me?

— Anne, listen a moment. . . . I fear. . . .

ANNE VERCORS: Well?

THE MOTHER: Mara

Slept in my room this winter, while you were ill,
and we talked at night in our beds.

Surely he is an honest lad, and I love him like
my own child, almost.

He has no property, that is true, but he is a good
ploughman, and comes of a good family.

We could give them

Our Demi-muids farm with the lower fields which
are too far away for us. — I, too, wanted to
speak to you of him.

ANNE VERCORS: Well?

THE MOTHER: Well, nothing.

No doubt Violaine is the eldest.

ANNE VERCORS: Come, come, what then?

THE MOTHER: What then? How do you know surely
that he loves her? —Our old friend, Master Pierre,

(Why did he keep away from us this time without
seeing anybody?)

You saw him last year when he came,

And how he looked at her while she served us. —
Certainly he has no land, but he earns much
money.

— And she, while he spoke,

How she listened to him, with her eyes wide
open like a child's,

Forgetting to pour the drink for us, so that I
had to scold her!

— And Mara, you know her. You know how
hard-headed she is!

If she has a notion then

That she will marry Jacques, — heigh-ho! She
is hard as iron.

I don't know! Perhaps it would be better . . .

ANNE VERCORS: What is all this nonsense?

THE MOTHER: Very well! Very well! we can talk like that. You must not get angry.

ANNE VERCORS: It is my will.

Jacques shall marry Violaine.

THE MOTHER: Well! he shall marry her then.

ANNE VERCORS: And now, mother, I have something else to tell you, poor old woman! I am going away.

THE MOTHER: You are going away? You are going away, old man? What is that you say?

ANNE VERCORS: That is why Jacques must marry Violaine without delay, and take my place here.

THE MOTHER: Lord! You are going away! You mean it? And where are you going?

ANNE VERCORS (*pointing vaguely toward the south*): Down there.

THE MOTHER: To Château?

ANNE VERCORS: Farther than Château.

THE MOTHER (*lowering her voice*): To Bourges, to the other King?

ANNE VERCORS: To the King of Kings, to Jerusalem.

THE MOTHER: Lord!   (*She sits down.*

Is it because France is not good enough for you?

ANNE VERCORS: There is too much sorrow in France.

THE MOTHER: But we are very comfortable here and nobody troubles Rheims.

ANNE VERCORS: That is it.

THE MOTHER: That is what?

ANNE VERCORS: The very thing; we are too happy,
And the others not happy enough.

THE MOTHER: Anne, that is not our fault.

ANNE VERCORS: It is not theirs either.

THE MOTHER: I don't know. I know that you are there and that I have two children.

ANNE VERCORS: But you see, surely, that everything is upset and put out of its right place, and everybody seeks distractedly to find where that place is.

And the smoke we see sometimes in the distance is not merely the smoke of burning straw.

And these crowds of poor people who come to us from every side.

There is no longer a King reigning over France, according to the prediction of the prophet.[1]

---

[1] "1 For, behold the Lord, the Lord of hosts, doth take away from Jerusalem and from Judah, the stay and the staff, the whole stay of bread, and the whole stay of water.

"2 The mighty man, and the man of war, the judge, and the prophet, and the prudent, and the ancient.

"3 The captain of fifty, and the honourable man, and the counsellor, and the cunning artificer, and the eloquent orator.

"4 And I will give children to be their princes, and babes shall rule over them." — Isaiah iii, 1–5.

THE MOTHER: That is what you read to us the other day?

ANNE VERCORS: In the place of the King we have two children.

The English one, in his island,

And the other one, so little that among the reeds of the Loire he cannot be seen.

In place of the Pope we have three Popes, and instead of Rome, I don't know what council or other in Switzerland.

All is struggling and moving,

Having no longer any counterweight to steady it.

THE MOTHER: And you, also, where do you want to go?

ANNE VERCORS: I can no longer stay here.

THE MOTHER: Anne, have I done anything to grieve you?

ANNE VERCORS: No, my Elisabeth.

THE MOTHER: Here you abandon me in my old age.

ANNE VERCORS: Give me leave to go, yourself.

THE MOTHER: You do not love me any more and you are no longer happy with me.

ANNE VERCORS: I am weary of being happy.

THE MOTHER: Scorn not the gift which God has given you.

ANNE VERCORS: God be praised who has overwhelmed me with his goodness!

For these thirty years now I have held this sacred
fief from my father, and God has sent rain
on my furrows.

For ten years there has not been one hour of
my work

That he has not repaid four times over and more,

As if it were not his will to keep open his account
with me, or leave anything owing.

All else perished, yet I was spared.

So that I shall appear before him empty and without a claim, among those who have received
their reward.

THE MOTHER: It is enough to have a grateful
heart.

ANNE VERCORS: But I am not satisfied with his
benefits,

And because I have received them, shall I leave
the greater good to others?

THE MOTHER: I do not understand you.

ANNE VERCORS: Which receives more, the full or
the empty vessel?

And which has need of the most water, the cis-
tern or the spring?

THE MOTHER: Ours is nearly dried up by this long
hot summer.

ANNE VERCORS: Such has been the evil of this
world, that each has wanted to enjoy his own
as if it had been created for him,

And not at all as if he had received it by the
will of God,

The lord his estate, the father his children,

The King his Kingdom and the scholar his rank.

That is why God has taken away from them all
these things which can be taken away,

And has sent to each man deliverance and
fasting.

And why is the portion of others not mine also?

THE MOTHER: You have your duty here with us.

ANNE VERCORS: Not if you will absolve me from it.

THE MOTHER: I will not absolve you.

ANNE VERCORS: You see that what I had to do is
done.

The two children are reared, and Jacques is
there to take my place.

THE MOTHER: Who calls you far away from us?

ANNE VERCORS (*smiling*): An angel blowing a
trumpet.

THE MOTHER: What trumpet?

ANNE VERCORS: The soundless trumpet that is
heard by all.

The trumpet that calls all men from time to time
that the portions may be distributed afresh.

The trumpet in the valley of Jehosaphat before
it has made a sound,

That of Bethlehem when Augustus numbered the
people.

The trumpet of the Assumption, when the apostles
  were assembled.

The voice which takes the place of the Word
  when the Chief no longer speaks

To the body that seeks union with him.

THE MOTHER: Jerusalem is so far away!

ANNE VERCORS: Paradise is still farther.

THE MOTHER: God in the tabernacle is with us
  even here.

ANNE VERCORS: But not that great hole in the earth.

THE MOTHER: What hole?

ANNE VERCORS: That the Cross made when it
  was set there.

Behold how it draws everything to itself.

There is the stitch which cannot be undone, the
  knot which cannot be untied,

The heritage of all, the interior boundary stone
  that can never be uprooted,

The centre and the navel of the world, the ele-
  ment by which all humanity is held together.

THE MOTHER: What can one pilgrim alone do?

ANNE VERCORS: I am not alone! A great multitude rejoice and depart with me!

The multitude of all my dead,

Those souls, one above the other, of whom nothing
  is left now but the tombstones, all those stones
  baptized with me who claim their rightful
  place in the structure!

35

And as it is true that the Christian is never alone,
  but is in communion with all his brothers,
The whole kingdom is with me, invoking, and
  drawing near to the Seat of God, taking anew
  its course toward him,
And I am its deputy and I carry it with me
To lay it once again upon the eternal Pattern.

THE MOTHER: Who knows but that we shall need
  you here?

ANNE VERCORS: Who knows but that I am needed
  elsewhere?

Everything is shaking; who knows but that I
  obstruct God's plan by remaining here
Where the need there was of me is past?

THE MOTHER: I know you are an inflexible man.

ANNE VERCORS (*tenderly, changing his voice*): To me
  you are always young and beautiful, and very
  great is the love I feel for my black-haired
  sweet Elisabeth.

THE MOTHER: My hair is grey!

ANNE VERCORS: Say yes, Elisabeth. . . .

THE MOTHER: Anne, you have not left me in all
  these thirty years. What will become of me
  without my chief and my companion?

ANNE VERCORS: . . . The yes which will separate
  us now, very low,
As round as the oui that formerly made us one.

(*Silence.*

THE MOTHER (*speaking very low*): Yes, Anne.

ANNE VERCORS: Have patience, Zabillet! I shall soon return.

Can you not have faith in me a little while, though I am not here!

Soon will come another separation.

Come, put food for two days in a bag. It is time I was off.

THE MOTHER: What? To-day, even to-day?

ANNE VERCORS: Even to-day.

> (*Her head droops and she does not move. He takes her in his arms but she does not respond.*)

Farewell, Elisabeth.

THE MOTHER: Alas, old man, I shall never see you again.

ANNE VERCORS: And now I must seek Jacques.

Act One: Scene Two

(Enter MARA.

MARA to THE MOTHER: Go, and tell him she is not to marry him.

THE MOTHER: Mara! How is this? You were there?

MARA: Go, I tell you, and tell him she is not to marry him.

THE MOTHER: What, she? What, he? What do you know of her marrying him?

MARA: I was there. I heard it all.

THE MOTHER: Very well, my child! Your father wishes it.

You have seen I did what I could, and his mind is not changed.

MARA: Go and tell him that she is not to marry him, or I will kill myself!

THE MOTHER: Mara!

MARA: I will hang myself in the wood-house, there where we found the cat hung.

THE MOTHER: Mara! Wicked girl!

MARA: There again she has taken him away from me! Now she has taken him away!

It was always I who was to be his wife, and not she.

She knows very well it is I.

THE MOTHER: She is the eldest.

MARA: What does that matter?

THE MOTHER: It is your father who wishes it.

MARA: I don't care.

THE MOTHER: Jacques Hury
Loves her.

MARA: That is not true! I know well enough
that you do not love me!

You have always loved her best! Oh, when you
talk of your Violaine it is like talking of sugar,

It is like sucking a cherry just when you are about
to spit out the stone!

But Mara the magpie! She is as hard as iron,
she is as sour as the wild cherry!

Added to that, there's always the talk of your
Violaine being so beautiful!

And behold, she is now to have Combernon!

What does she know how to do, the ferret?
which of us two can drive the cart?

She thinks herself like Saint Onzemillevierges!
But, as for me, I am Mara Vercors, who hates
injustice and deceit,

Mara who speaks the truth and it is that which
makes the servants angry!

Let them be angry! I scorn them. Not one of
the women dares stir in my presence, the hypo-
crites! Everything goes as smoothly as at the
mill.

—And yet everything is for her and nothing for me.

THE MOTHER: You will have your share.

MARA: Aye, truly! The sandy ground up yonder! ooze and mud that it needs five oxen to plough! the bad ground of Chinchy.

THE MOTHER: It brings in good profit all the same.

MARA: Surely.

Long-rooted reeds and cow-wheat, senna, and mullein!

I shall have enough to make my herb-tea.

THE MOTHER: Bad girl; you know well enough that is not true!

You know well no wrong is done you!

But you have always been wicked! When you were little

You would not cry when you were beaten.

Tell me, you black-skinned child, you ugly one!

Is she not the eldest?

What have you against her?

Jealous girl! Yet she has always done what you wish.

Very well! She will be married first, and you will be married, you also, afterwards!

And it is too late to do differently anyhow, because your father is going away — oh, how sad I am!

He has gone to speak to Violaine and he will
look for Jacques.

MARA: That's true! Go at once! Go, go at
once!

THE MOTHER: Go where?

MARA: Mother, come now! You know well I
am the one. Tell him she is not to marry him,
maman!

THE MOTHER: Surely I shall do no such thing.

MARA: Only tell him what I have said. Tell him
that I will kill myself. Do you understand?

(*She looks fixedly at her.*

THE MOTHER: Ha!

MARA: Do you believe I will not do it?

THE MOTHER: Alack, I know you would!

MARA: Go then!

THE MOTHER: O
Obstinate!

MARA: You have nothing to do with it.
Only to repeat to him just what I have
said.

THE MOTHER: And he — how do you know he will
be willing to marry you?

MARA: Certainly he will not.

THE MOTHER: Well. . . .

MARA: Well?

THE MOTHER: Don't think that I shall advise him
to do your will! — on the contrary!

I will only tell him what you have said. It is
  very sure
That she will not be so silly as to give in to you,
  if she will listen to me.

MARA: Perhaps. — Go. — Do as I say.

(She goes out.

Act One: Scene Three

(Enter ANNE VERCORS *and* JACQUES HURY, *afterwards* VIOLAINE, *and then the farm labourers and servants.*

ANNE VERCORS *(stopping)*: Heh! what is that thou tell'st me?

JACQUES HURY: Just as I say! This time I took him in the act, with the pruning-hook in his hand!

I came up softly behind him and all of a sudden

Flac! I threw myself full length on him,

As you throw yourself on a hare in her hole at harvest

And there beside him was a bunch of twenty young poplars, the ones you set such store by!

ANNE VERCORS: Why did he not come to me? I should have given him the wood he needed.

JACQUES HURY: The wood he needs is the handle of my whip!

It is not need but wickedness, the idea of doing wrong!

These ne'er-do-wells from Chevoche are always ready to do anything

43

Out of bravado, and to defy people!

But as to that man, I will cut off his ears with my little knife!

ANNE VERCORS: No.

JACQUES HURY: At least let me tie him by his wrists to the harrow, before the big gate,

With his face turned against the teeth; with Faraud the dog to watch him.

ANNE VERCORS: Not that either.

JACQUES HURY: What is to be done then?

ANNE VERCORS: Send him home.

JACQUES HURY: With his bundle of wood?

ANNE VERCORS: And with another that thou wilt give him.

JACQUES HURY: Father, that is not right.

ANNE VERCORS: Thou canst tie his faggot around, that he may not lose any of it.

That will help him in crossing the ford at Saponay.

JACQUES HURY: It is not well to be lax about one's rights.

ANNE VERCORS: I know it, it is not well!

Jacques, behold how lazy and old I am, weary of fighting and defending.

Once I was harsh like thee.

There is a time to take and a time to let take.

The budding tree must be protected, but the tree where the fruit hangs do not trouble thyself about.

44

Let us be unjust in very little, lest God be unjust to me in much.

— And besides, thou wilt do now as thou wilt,
for thou art placed over Combernon in my
stead.

JACQUES HURY: What do you say?

THE MOTHER: He is going a pilgrim to Jerusalem.

JACQUES HURY: Jerusalem?

ANNE VERCORS: It is true. I start this very
moment.

JACQUES HURY: What? What does that mean?

ANNE VERCORS: Thou hast heard very well.

JACQUES HURY: Thou wilt leave us like that, when
the work is at its heaviest?

ANNE VERCORS: It is not necessary to have two
masters at Combernon.

JACQUES HURY: My father, I am only your son!

ANNE VERCORS: Thou wilt be the father here,
in my stead.

JACQUES HURY: I do not understand you.

ANNE VERCORS: I am going away. Take Combernon from me

As I took it from my father, and he from his,

And Radulphe the Frank, first of our line, from
Saint Rémy de Rheims,

Who from Genevieve of Paris received this land,
pagan and bristling with seedlings and wild
thorns.

45

Radulphe and his children made it Christian by
iron and by fire

And laid it naked and broken under the waters
of baptism.

Hill and plain scored they with equal furrows,

As an industrious scholar copies line after line
the word of God.

And they began to build Monsanvierge on the
mountain, in that place where Evil was wor-
shipped,

(And at first there was naught but a cabin made
of logs and reeds, whose door the Bishop came
to seal,

And two holy recluses were left to guard it),

And at the mountain's base, Combernon, a dwelling
armed and provisioned.

Thus this land is free that we hold from St.
Rémy in heaven, paying tithes up there to
this flight, one moment stayed, of murmuring
doves.

For everything is of God, and those who live in
Him reap without ceasing the fruits of their
works,

Which pass and come back to us again in their
time in magnificent succession;

As over the various harvests every day in summer
float those great clouds that drift toward
Germany.

The cattle here are never sick, the udders and
the wells are never dry; the grain is as solid
as gold, the straw as firm as iron.

And for defence against pillagers we have arms,
and the walls of Combernon, and the King,
our neighbor.

Gather this harvest that I have sown, as in the
past I myself have filled again the furrows my
father ploughed.

O joyful work of the farmer, for which the sun
is as bright as our glistening ox, and the rain
is our banker, and God works with us every
day, making of everything the best!

Others look to men for their rewards, but we
receive ours straight from heaven itself,

A hundred for one, the full ear for a seed, and
the tree for a nut.

For such is the justice of God to us, and the
measure with which He repays us.

The earth cleaves to the sky, the body to the
spirit, all things that He has created are in
communion, all have need of one another.

Take the handles of the plough in my stead, that
the earth may bring forth bread as God himself has wished.

Give food to all creatures, men and animals, to
spirits and bodies, and to immortal souls.

You, women, labourers, look! Behold the son

I have chosen, Jacques! I am going away and
he stays in my place. Obey him.

JACQUES HURY: May it be done according to your
will.

ANNE VERCORS: Violaine!

My child, first born instead of the son I have
not had!

Heir of my name in whom I too shall be given
to another!

Violaine, when thou shalt have a husband, do not
scorn the love of thy father.

For thou canst not give back to a father what
he has given thee, when thou wouldst.

Between husband and wife everything is equal;
what they do not know they accept, one from
the other, with faith.

This is the mutual religion, this is the servitude
through which the wife's breast grows large
with milk!

But the father, seeing his children separate from
him, recognizes what was once within himself. My daughter, know thy father!

A Father's love

Asks no return, and the child has no need either
to win or merit it:

As it was his before the beginning, so it remains

His blessing and his inheritance, his help, his
honour, his right, his justification!

My soul is never divided from the soul I have
transmitted.

What I have given can never be given back. Only
know, O my child, that I am thy father!

And of my issue there is no male. Only women
have I brought into the world.

Nothing but that thing in us which gives and
which is given.

—And now the hour of parting is come.

VIOLAINE: Father! Do not say such a cruel thing!

ANNE VERCORS: Jacques, you are the man whom I
love. Take her! I give you my daughter,
Violaine. Take my name from her.

Love her, for she is as pure as gold.

All the days of thy life, like bread, of which one
never tires.

She is simple and obedient, sensitive and reserved.

Do not cause her any sorrow, and give her only
kindness.

Everything here is thine, except what will be
given to Mara, in accordance with my plan.

JACQUES HURY: What, my father, your daughter,
your property . . .

ANNE VERCORS: I give you all at once, as all is
mine.

JACQUES HURY: But who knows if she still cares
for me?

ANNE VERCORS: Who knows?

> (*She looks at* JACQUES *and forms* "Yes"
> *with her lips, without speaking.*

JACQUES HURY: You care for me, Violaine?

VIOLAINE: My father wishes it.

JACQUES HURY: You wish it too?

VIOLAINE: I wish it too.

JACQUES HURY: Violaine!

How shall we get on together?

VIOLAINE: Consider well while there is yet time!

JACQUES HURY: Then I take you by God's command, and I will nevermore let you go.

> (*He takes her by both hands.*

I have you and hold you, your hand and the arm with it, and all that comes with the arm.

Parents, your daughter is no longer yours! She is mine only!

ANNE VERCORS: Well, they are married; it is done! What say you, mother?

THE MOTHER: I am very glad!　　　(*She weeps.*

ANNE VERCORS: She weeps, my wife!

There! that is how they take our children from us and we shall be left alone,

The old woman who lives on a little milk and a small bit of cake,

And the old man with his ears full of white hairs like the heart of an artichoke.

—Let them make ready the wedding-dress!

—Children, I shall not be at your wedding.

VIOLAINE: What, father!

THE MOTHER: Anne!

ANNE VERCORS: I am going. Now.

VIOLAINE: O father! before we are married.

ANNE VERCORS: It must be. Your mother will
explain all to you.   (*Enter* MARA.

THE MOTHER: How long shall you stay over there?

ANNE VERCORS: I do not know. It may be but
a short time.

I shall soon be coming back.   (*Silence.*

VOICE OF A CHILD (*in the distance*): Oriole, oriole!
all alone!

Who eats the wild cherry and throws out the stone!

ANNE VERCORS: The oriole, rosy and golden, whistles
in the heart of the tree.

What does he say? that after these long days of
heat

The rain last night was like a shower of gold
falling upon the earth.

What does he say? he says it is good weather
for ploughing.

What more does he say? that the weather is fine,
that God is great, and that it is still two hours
of noon.

What more does the little bird say?

That it is time for the old man to go

Elsewhere, and leave the world to itself.

—Jacques, I leave to you all my property, — protect these women.

JACQUES HURY: What, are you really going?

ANNE VERCORS: I believe he has heard nothing.

JACQUES HURY: Like that, right away?

ANNE VERCORS: The hour is come.

THE MOTHER: You will not go without first eating?
> (*During this time the women servants have prepared the table for the farm meal.*

ANNE VERCORS: (*to a woman servant*): Ho! my bag, my hat!

Bring my shoes! bring my cloak!

I have not time enough to share this meal with you.

THE MOTHER: Anne! How long wilt thou stay over there? One year, two years? More than two years?

ANNE VERCORS: One year. Two years. Yes, that is it.

Put on my shoes.
> (THE MOTHER *kneels before him and puts on his shoes.*

For the first time I leave thee, O house!

Combernon, lofty dwelling!

Watch faithfully over it all! Jacques will be here in my stead.

There is the hearth where there is always fire, there is the long table where I give food to my people.

All take your places! Just once more I will cut
the bread. . . .

> (*He seats himself at the head of the long
> table, with* THE MOTHER *at his right.
> All the men and women servants stand,
> each at his place.*
>
> *He takes the bread, making the sign of the
> cross above it with the knife, and cuts it;
> and gives it to* VIOLAINE *and* MARA *to
> pass. The last piece he keeps himself.
> Then he turns solemnly toward* THE MOTHER
> *and opens his arms.*

Farewell, Elisabeth!

THE MOTHER (*weeping in his arms*): Thou wilt
never see me more.

ANNE VERCORS (*in a lower tone*): Farewell, Elisabeth.

> (*He turns toward* MARA, *looks gravely at
> her for a long time, and then holds out his
> hand to her.*

Farewell, Mara! be virtuous.

MARA (*kissing his hand*): Farewell, father!

> (*Silence.* ANNE VERCORS *stands, looking
> before him as if he did not see* VIOLAINE, *who
> stands full of agitation at his side. At
> last he turns slightly toward her, and she
> puts her arms around his neck, sobbing,
> with her face against his breast.*

ANNE VERCORS (*to the men servants, as if he noticed nothing*): Farewell, all!

I have always dealt justly by you. If any one denies this, he lies.

I am not like other masters. But I praise when praise is due, and I reprove when reproof is due.

Now that I am going away, do your duty as if I were there.

For I shall return. I shall return some time when you do not expect me.

> (*He shakes hands with them all.*

Let my horse be brought!

> (*Silence. He leans toward* VIOLAINE, *who continues to embrace him.*

What is it, little child?

You have exchanged a husband for thy father.

VIOLAINE: Alas! Father! Alas!

> (*He removes her hands gently from around his neck.*

THE MOTHER: Tell me when will you return.

ANNE VERCORS: I cannot tell.

Perhaps it will be in the morning, perhaps at mid-day, when you are eating.

And perhaps, awaking some night, you will hear my step on the road.

Farewell! (*He goes.*

Act Two: Scene One

A fortnight later. The beginning of July. Noon.
A large orchard planted with regular rows of round
trees. Higher, and a little withdrawn, the wall and
towers and long buildings with tiled roofs of Combernon.
Then, the side of the hill, which rises abruptly, and on
its summit the massive stone arch of Monsanvierge,
without door or window, with its five towers like those
of the Cathedral of Laon, and in its side the great white
scar made for the recent entrance of the Queen Mother
of France.
Everything vibrates under an ardent sun.

A WOMAN's VOICE on high, from the height of the
    highest tower of Monsanvierge.

SALVE REGINA MATER MISERICORDIÆ

VITA DULCEDO ET SPES NOSTRA SALVE

AD TE CLAMAMUS EXULES FILII HEVÆ

AD TE SUSPIRAMUS GEMENTES ET FLENTES IN HAC
    LACRYMARUM VALLE

EIA ERGO ADVOCATA NOSTRA ILLOS TUOS MISERI-
    CORDES OCULOS AD NOS CONVERTE

ET JESUM BENEDICTUM FRUCTUM VENTRIS TUI NOBIS
    POST HOC EXILIUM OSTENDE

O CLEMENS

O PIA

O DULCIS VIRGO MARIA

> (*Long pause during which the stage remains empty.*

> (*Enter* THE MOTHER *and* MARA.

MARA: What did she say?

THE MOTHER: I drew her out as we talked, without seeming to. You see how she has lost her gay spirits these last few days.

MARA: She never talks much.

THE MOTHER: But she does not laugh any more. That troubles me.

Perhaps it is because Jacquin is away, but he returns to-day.

—And her father too is gone.

MARA: That is all thou said to her?

THE MOTHER: That is what I said to her, and the rest of it without changing a word, just as you said it to me: Jacquin and you: that you love him and all.

And I added, and I said it over two or three times, that this time she must not be foolish, and not resist at all,

Or break off the marriage, which is as good as made, against the father's will.

What would people think of it?

MARA: And what did she answer?

THE MOTHER: She began to laugh, and I, I began to cry.

56

MARA: I will make her laugh!

THE MOTHER: It was not the laughter I love of my little girl, and I began to cry.

And I said, "No, no, Violaine, my child!" not knowing any longer what I said.

But she, without speaking, made a sign with her hand that she wanted to be alone.

Ah! what misery we have with our children!

MARA: Hush!

THE MOTHER: What is it?

I am sorry for what I have done.

MARA: Well! Do you see her down there in the paddock? She is walking behind the trees. Now she is out of sight.

(*Silence. From behind the scene is heard the blast of a horn.*

THE MOTHER: There is Jacquin come back. I know the sound of his horn.

MARA: Let us go further off.   (*They move off.*

Act Two: Scene Two

> (*Enter* JACQUES HURY.

JACQUES HURY (*looking all around*): I don't see
  her.
  And yet she sent word
  That she wanted to see me this morning,
  Here.

> (*Enter* MARA. *She advances to* JACQUES,
> *and at six paces before him drops a cere-*
> *monious courtesy.*

JACQUES HURY: Good morning, Mara.

MARA: My lord, your servant!

JACQUES HURY: What is this foolery?

MARA: Do I not owe you respect? Are you not
  the master here, dependent only upon God,
  like the King of France himself and the Emperor Charlemagne?

JACQUES HURY: Jest if you like, but it is true
  all the same! Yes, Mara, it is glorious! Dear
  sister, I am too happy!

MARA: I am not your *dear* sister! I am your
  servant because I must be.
  Man of Braine! son of a serf! I am not your
  sister; you are not of our blood!

JACQUES HURY: I am the husband of Violaine.

58

MARA: You are not that yet.

JACQUES HURY: I shall be to-morrow.

MARA: Who knows?

JACQUES HURY: Mara, I have thought deeply about it,

And I believe you have only dreamed that story you told me the other day.

MARA: What story?

JACQUES HURY: Don't pretend not to know.

That story about the mason, that secret kiss at dawn.

MARA: It is possible. I did not see well. Yet I have good eyes.

JACQUES HURY: And it has been whispered to me that the man is a leper!

MARA: I do not love you, Jacques.

But you have the right to know all. All must be pure and clear at Monsanvierge, which is held up like a monstrance before all the kingdom.

JACQUES HURY: All that will be explained in a moment.

MARA: You are clever and nothing can escape you.

JACQUES HURY: I see at any rate that you don't love me.

MARA: There! there! What did I say? what did I say?

JACQUES HURY: Everybody here is not of your
mind.

MARA: You speak of Violaine? I blush for that
little girl.

It is shameful to give oneself like that,

Soul, body, heart, skin, the outside, the inside,
and the root.

JACQUES HURY: I know that she belongs entirely
to me.

MARA: Yes.

How grandly he speaks! how sure he is of the
things that belong to him! Brainard of Braine!

Only those things belong to one that one has
made, or taken, or earned.

JACQUES HURY: But Mara, I like you, and I have
nothing against you.

MARA: Without doubt — like all the rest of the
things here?

JACQUES HURY: It is no fault of mine that you
are not a man, and that I take your property
from you!

MARA: How proud and satisfied he is! Look at him,
he can hardly keep from laughing!

There now! don't do yourself harm! Laugh!

(*He laughs.*

I know your face well, Jacques.

JACQUES HURY: You are angry because you cannot
make me unhappy.

60

MARA: Like the other day while the father was talking,

When one of your eyes smiled and the other wept — without tears.

JACQUES HURY: Am I not master of a fine estate?

MARA: And the father was old, wasn't he? You know a thing or two more than he does?

JACQUES HURY: To each man his day.

MARA: That is true, Jacques, you are a tall and handsome young man.

See him, how he blushes.

JACQUES HURY: Don't torment me.

MARA: All the same, it is a pity!

JACQUES HURY: What is a pity?

MARA: Farewell, husband of Violaine! Farewell, master of Monsanvierge — ah — ah!

JACQUES HURY: I will show you that so I am.

MARA: Then understand the spirit of this place, Brainard of Braine!

He thinks that everything is his, like a peasant; you will be shown the contrary!

Like a peasant who sees nothing higher than himself as he stands in the midst of his flat little field!

But Monsanvierge belongs to God, and the master of Monsanvierge is God's man, who has nothing

For himself, having received everything for another.

61

That is the lesson passed on here from father to
  son. There is no higher position than ours.
Take on the spirit of your masters, peasant!
      (*She makes as if to go and turns back.*
Ah!
Violaine, when I met her,
Gave me a message for you.
JACQUES HURY: Why did you not say so sooner?
MARA: She is waiting for you near the fountain.

Act Two: Scene Three

The fountain of the Adoue. It is a large square orifice cut in a vertical wall, built of blocks of limestone. A thin stream of water drips from it with a melancholy sound. Thank-offerings of crosses made of straw and bouquets of faded flowers are hung on the wall.

The fountain is surrounded with luxurious trees, and with a bower of rose-bushes whose abundant blossoms thickly star the green foliage.

JACQUES HURY (*he looks at* VIOLAINE *who comes along the winding path. She is all golden, and glows brilliantly at moments when the sun falls upon her between the leaves*): O my betrothed among the flowery branches, hail!

        (VIOLAINE *enters and stands before him. She is clothed in a linen gown with a kind of dalmatic of cloth-of-gold decorated with large red and blue flowers. Her head is crowned with a diadem of enamel and gold.*

Violaine, how beautiful you are!

VIOLAINE: Jacques! Good morning, Jacques! Ah, how long you stayed down there!

JACQUES HURY: I had to get rid of everything, and sell, in order to be perfectly free.

To be the man of Monsanvierge only and yours.

—What is this wonderful dress?

VIOLAINE: I wore it for you. I had spoken to you about it. Do you not recognize it?

It is the habit of the nuns of Monsanvierge, except only the maniple, the habit they wear in the choir,

The deacon's dalmatic which they have the privilege of wearing, something priestly, as they themselves are holy sacrifices,

And the women of Combernon have the right to wear it twice:

First, on the day of their betrothal,

Secondly, on the day of their death.

JACQUES HURY: It is really true, then, that this is the day of our betrothal, Violaine?

VIOLAINE: Jacques, there is yet time, we are not married yet!

If you have only wanted to please my father there is still time to withdraw; it concerns no one but us. Say but a word, and I would not want you any more, Jacques.

For nothing has yet been put in writing, and I do not know if I still please you.

JACQUES HURY: How beautiful you are, Violaine! And how beautiful is the world of which you are the portion reserved for me.

VIOLAINE: It is you, Jacques, who are all that is best in the world.

JACQUES HURY: Is it true that you are willing to belong to me?

VIOLAINE: Yes, it is true! good morning, my beloved! I am yours.

JACQUES HURY: Good morning, my wife! Good morning, sweet Violaine!

VIOLAINE: These are good things to hear, Jacques!

JACQUES HURY: You must always be there! Tell me that you will always be the same, the angel who is sent to me!

VIOLAINE: For evermore all that is mine shall always be yours.

JACQUES HURY: And as for me, Violaine. . . .

VIOLAINE: Say nothing. I ask you nothing. You are there, and that is enough for me. Good morning, Jacques!
Ah, how beautiful this hour is, and I ask for nothing more.

JACQUES HURY: To-morrow will be still more beautiful!

VIOLAINE: To-morrow I shall have taken off my gorgeous robe.

JACQUES HURY: But you will be so near to me that I shall no longer be able to see you.

VIOLAINE: Very near to you indeed!

JACQUES HURY: Your place is ready.
Violaine, what a solitary spot this is, and how secretly I am here with you!

VIOLAINE (*in a low tone*): Your heart is enough. Go to, I am with you, and say not a word more.

JACQUES HURY: But to-morrow, before everybody, I will take this Queen in my arms.

VIOLAINE: Take her, and do not let her go.

Ah, take your little one with you so that they can never find her, and never do her any harm!

JACQUES HURY: And you will not regret then the linen and the gold?

VIOLAINE: Was I wrong to make myself beautiful for one poor little hour?

JACQUES HURY: No, my beautiful lily, I can never tire of looking at you in your glory!

VIOLAINE: O Jacques! tell me again that you think me beautiful!

JACQUES HURY: Yes, Violaine!

VIOLAINE: The most beautiful of all, and the other women are nothing to you?

JACQUES HURY: Yes, Violaine.

VIOLAINE: And that you love me only, as the tenderest husband loves the poor creature who has given herself to him?

JACQUES HURY: Yes, Violaine.

VIOLAINE: Who gives herself to him with all her heart, Jacques, believe me, and holds nothing back.

JACQUES HURY: And you, Violaine, do you not believe me then?

VIOLAINE: I believe you, I believe you, Jacques!
I believe in you! I have confidence in you,
my darling!

JACQUES HURY: Why, then, do you seem troubled
and frightened?
Show me your left hand. (*She shows it.*
My ring is gone.

VIOLAINE: I will explain that to you presently,
you will be satisfied.

JACQUES HURY: I am satisfied, Violaine. I have
faith in you.

VIOLAINE: I am more than a ring, Jacques. I
am a great treasure.

JACQUES HURY: Yes, Violaine.

VIOLAINE: Ah, if I give myself to you,
Will you not know how to save your little one
who loves you?

JACQUES HURY: There you are doubting me again.

VIOLAINE: Jacques! After all I do no harm in
loving you. It is God's will, and my father's.
It is you who have charge of me! And who
knows if you will not know perfectly how to
defend and save me?
It is enough that I give myself entirely to you.
The rest is your affair, and no longer mine.

JACQUES HURY: And is it like this you give yourself to me, my flower-o'-the-sun?

VIOLAINE: Yes, Jacques.

JACQUES HURY: Who then can take you out of my
arms?

VIOLAINE: Ah, how big the world is, and how
alone we are!

JACQUES HURY: Poor child! I know that your
father is gone.

And I too no longer have anyone with me to
tell me what should be done, and what is good
or ill.

You must help me, Violaine, as I love you.

VIOLAINE: My father has abandoned me.

JACQUES HURY: But I remain to you, Violaine.

VIOLAINE: Neither my mother nor my sister love
me, though I have done them no wrong.

And nothing is left to me but this tall, terrible
man whom I do not know.

(*He tries to take her in his arms. She
pushes him away quickly.*

Do not touch me, Jacques!

JACQUES HURY: Am I then a leper?

VIOLAINE: Jacques, I want to speak to you —
ah, but it is hard!

Do not fail me, who now have only you!

JACQUES HURY: Who would do you harm?

VIOLAINE: Know what you do in taking me for
your wife!

Let me speak to you very humbly, my lord
Jacques,

Who are about to receive my soul and my body
from the hands of God according to his command, and my father's who made them.

And know the dowry I bring to you which is not
like those of other women,

But this holy mountain wrapped in prayer day
and night before God, like an altar smoking
always,

And this lamp whose light is never suffered to
go out, and whose oil it is our duty to replenish.

And no man is witness to our marriage, but that
Lord whose fief we alone hold,

Who is the Omnipotent, the God of the Armies.

And it is not the sun of July that lights us, but
the light of his countenance.

To the holy be the holy things! Who knows if
our heart be pure?

Never until now has a male been lacking to our
race, and always the sacred place has been
handed down from father to son,

And behold, for the first time it falls into the
hands of a woman, and becomes with her
the object of desire.

JACQUES HURY: Violaine — no: I am not a scholar
nor a monk nor a saint.

I am not the lay-servant of Monsanvierge, nor
the keeper of its turning-box.

I have a duty and I will perform it,

69

Which is to feed these murmuring birds,
And to fill each morning the basket they lower
from the sky.
That is written down. That is right.
I have understood that, and I have fixed it in
my head, and you must not ask any more
of me.
You must not ask me to understand what is
above me, and why these holy women have
imprisoned themselves up there in that pigeon-
house.
To the heavenly be heaven, and the earth to the
earthly.
For the wheat will not grow by itself, and a good
ploughman is necessary.
And I can say without boasting that such I am,
and no one can teach me that, not even your
father himself perhaps,
For he was old and set in his ways.
To each one his own place, and that is justice.
And your father, in giving you to me,
Together with Monsanvierge, knew what he was
doing, and that was just.

VIOLAINE: But Jacques, I do not love you because it is just.
And even if it were not just, I would love you
the same, and more.

JACQUES HURY: I do not understand you, Violaine.

VIOLAINE: Jacques, do not make me speak! You love me so much, and I can only do you harm. Let me alone! there cannot be justice between us two! but only faith and charity. Go away from me while there is yet time.

JACQUES HURY: I do not understand, Violaine.

VIOLAINE: My beloved, do not force me to tell you my great secret.

JACQUES HURY: A great secret, Violaine?

VIOLAINE: So great that all is over, and you will not ask to marry me any more.

JACQUES HURY: I do not understand you.

VIOLAINE: Am I not beautiful enough just now, Jacques? What more do you ask of me?

What does one ask of a flower

Except to be beautiful and fragrant for a moment, poor flower, and then — the end.

The flower's life is short, but the joy it has given for a minute

Is not of those things which have a beginning and an end.

Am I not beautiful enough? Is something lacking? Ah! I see thine eyes, my beloved! Is there anything in thee at this moment that does not love me, and that doubts me?

Is my soul not enough? Take it, and I am still here, and absorb to its depths that which is all thine!

To die requires but a moment, and to die in
each other would not annihilate us more than
love, and does one need to live when one is
dead?

What more wouldst thou do with me? Fly, take
thyself away! Why dost thou wish to marry
me? Why dost thou wish

To take for thyself what belongs only to God?

The hand of God is upon us, and thou canst not
defend me!

O Jacques, we shall never be husband and wife
in this world!

JACQUES HURY: Violaine, what are these strange
words, so tender, so bitter? By what threat-
ening and gloomy paths are you leading me?

I believe you wish to put me to the proof, and
to triumph over me, who am but a simple and
rough man.

Ah! Violaine, how beautiful you are like this!
and yet I am afraid, and I see you in clothing
that terrifies me!

For this is not a woman's dress, but the robe of
one who offers the sacrifice at the altar,

Of him who waits upon the priest, leaving the
side uncovered and the arms free!

Ah, I see, it is the spirit of Monsanvierge which
lives in you, the supreme flower outside of this
sealed garden!

Ah, do not turn to me that face which is no
longer of this world! that is no longer my
dear Violaine.

There are enough angels to serve the mass in
Heaven!

Have pity on me, who am only a man without
wings, who rejoiced in this companion God
had given me, and that I should hear her sigh
with her head resting on my shoulder!

Sweet bird! the sky is beautiful, but it is beautiful too to be taken captive!

And the sky is beautiful! but this is a beautiful
thing too, and even worthy of God, the heart of
a man that can be filled, leaving no part empty.

Do not torment me by depriving me of your face!

And no doubt I am a dull and ugly man,

But I love you, my angel, my queen, my darling!

VIOLAINE: So I have warned you in vain, and you
want to take me for your wife, and you will
not give up your plan?

JACQUES HURY: Yes, Violaine.

VIOLAINE: When a man takes a woman for his
wife they are then one soul in one body, and
nothing will ever separate them.

JACQUES HURY: Yes, Violaine.

VIOLAINE: You wish it!

Then it is not right that I should reserve anything,
or keep to myself any longer

73

This great, this unspeakable secret.

JACQUES HURY: Again this secret, Violaine?

VIOLAINE: So great, truly, Jacques,
That your heart will be saturated with it,
And you will ask nothing more of me,
And that we shall never be torn apart from each
other.
A secret so deep
That neither life, Jacques, nor hell, nor Heaven
itself
Will ever end it, or will ever end this
Moment in which I have revealed it, here in the
burning
Heat of this terrible sun which almost prevents
us from seeing each other!

JACQUES HURY: Speak, then!

VIOLAINE: But tell me first once more that you
love me.

JACQUES HURY: I love you!

VIOLAINE: And that I am your wife and your
only love?

JACQUES HURY: My wife, my only love.

VIOLAINE: Tell me, Jacques: neither my face nor my
soul has sufficed thee, and that is not enough?
And have you been misled by my proud words?
Then learn of the fire which consumes me!
Know this flesh which you have loved so much!
Come nearer to me.   (*He comes nearer.*

Nearer! nearer still! close against my side. Sit
down on that bench.   (*Silence.*
And give me your knife.

> (*He gives her his knife. She cuts the linen
> of her gown, at her side upon the heart,
> under the left breast, and leaning towards
> him she opens the slit with her hands and
> shows him the flesh where the first spot of
> leprosy has appeared. Silence.*

JACQUES HURY (*slightly turning away his face*):
Give me the knife.

> (*She gives it to him. Silence. Then Jacques
> moves a few steps away from her, half
> turning his back, and he does not look at
> her again until the end of the Act.*

JACQUES HURY: Violaine, I am not mistaken?
What is this silver flower emblazoned
on your flesh?

VIOLAINE: You are not mistaken.

JACQUES HURY: It is the malady? it is the malady,
Violaine?

VIOLAINE: Yes, Jacques.

JACQUES HURY: Leprosy!

VIOLAINE: Surely you are hard to convince.
And you had to see it to believe.

JACQUES HURY: And which leprosy is the most
hideous,
That of the soul or that of the body?

VIOLAINE: I cannot say as to the other. I only know that of the body, which is bad enough.

JACQUES HURY: No, you know not the other, reprobate?

VIOLAINE: I am not a reprobate.

JACQUES HURY: Infamous woman, reprobate, Infamous in your soul and in your flesh!

VIOLAINE: So you do not ask any more to marry me, Jacques?

JACQUES HURY: Scoff no more, child of the devil!

VIOLAINE: Such is that great love you had for me.

JACQUES HURY: Such is this lily that I had chosen.

VIOLAINE: Such is the man who takes the place of my father.

JACQUES HURY: Such is the angel that God had sent me.

VIOLAINE: Ah, who will tear us apart from each other? I love you, Jacques, and you will defend me, and I know that in thy arms I have nothing to fear.

JACQUES HURY: Do not mock thyself with these horrible words!

VIOLAINE: Tell me,
Have I broken my word? My soul was not enough for thee? Have you enough now of my flesh?
Will you forget henceforth your Violaine, and the heart she revealed to thee?

JACQUES HURY: Go farther away from me!

VIOLAINE: Go to, I am far enough away, Jacques;
you have nothing to fear.

JACQUES HURY: Yes, yes,
Further than you were from that measled pig of
yours!
That maker of bones whereon the flesh rots!

VIOLAINE: Is it of Pierre de Craon that you speak?

JACQUES HURY: It is of him I speak, him you kissed
on the mouth.

VIOLAINE: And who has told you that?

JACQUES HURY: Mara saw you with her own eyes.
And she has told me all, as it was her duty to do,
And I, fool that I was, did not believe it!
Come, confess it! confess it then! It is true!
Say that it is true!

VIOLAINE: It is true, Jacques.
Mara always speaks the truth.

JACQUES HURY: And it is true that you kissed him
on the face?

VIOLAINE: It is true.

JACQUES HURY: O damned one! are the flames
of hell so savory that you have thus lusted
after them while you were still alive?

VIOLAINE (*speaking very low*): No, not damned.
But sweet, sweet Violaine! sweet, sweet Violaine!

JACQUES HURY: And you do not deny that this
man had you and possessed you?

VIOLAINE: I deny nothing, Jacques.

JACQUES HURY: But I love you still, Violaine! Ah, this is too cruel!
Tell me something, even if you have nothing to say, and I will believe it! Speak, I beg you! tell me it is not true!

VIOLAINE: I cannot turn all black in a minute, Jacques; but in a few months, a few months more,
You will not recognize me any longer.

JACQUES HURY: Tell me that all this is not true.

VIOLAINE: Mara always speaks the truth, and then there is that flower upon my body that you have seen.

JACQUES HURY: Farewell, Violaine.

VIOLAINE: Farewell, Jacques.

JACQUES HURY: Tell me, what shall you do, wretched woman?

VIOLAINE: Take off this robe. Leave this house. Fulfil the law. Show myself to the priest. Go to . . .

JACQUES HURY: Well?

VIOLAINE: . . . the place set apart for people like me.
The lazar-house of the Géyn, over there.

JACQUES HURY: When?

VIOLAINE: To-day — this very evening.

(Long silence.

There is nothing else to be done.

JACQUES HURY: We must avoid any scandal. Go, take off your robe and put on a travelling dress, and I will tell you what it is right to do.   (*They go out.*

Act Two: Scene Four

The kitchen at Combernon, as in ACT I

THE MOTHER: Every day the weather is fine.
It has not rained for eight days.   (*She listens.*
Now and then I hear the bells of Arcy.
Dong! Dong!
How warm it is, and how large everything looks!
What is Violaine doing? and Jacques? What
     have they to talk about so long?
I am sorry for what I said to her   (*She sighs.*
And what is the crazy old man doing? Where
     is he now?
Ah!   (*She bows her head.*
MARA (*entering quickly*): They are coming here. I
     think the marriage is broken off.   Do you hear
     me?
Be silent,
And say nothing.
THE MOTHER: What?
O wicked girl! wretch! You have got what
     you wished for!
MARA: Let it alone. It is only for a moment.
There was no other way
It could be done.   So, now it is I

He must marry and not she. It will be better
for her like that. It must be thus. Do you
hear?

Be silent!

THE MOTHER: Who told you that?

MARA: Was there need for me to be told? I saw
it all in their faces.

I came upon them all warm. I understood
everything in no time at all.

And Jacques, poor fellow, I pity him.

THE MOTHER: I am sorry for what I said!

MARA: You have said nothing; you know nothing —
be silent!

And if they say anything to you, no matter what
they tell you,

Agree with them, do everything they wish. There
is nothing more to do.

THE MOTHER: I hope all is for the best.

Act Two: Scene Five

(*Enter* JACQUES HURY, *then* VIOLAINE *all in
black, dressed as for a journey.*

THE MOTHER: What is the matter, Jacques? What
is the matter, Violaine?

Why have you put on this dress, as if you were
going away?

VIOLAINE: I, too, am going away.

THE MOTHER: Going away? You going away, too?
Jacques! what has happened between you?

JACQUES HURY: Nothing has happened.

But you know that I went to see my mother at
Braine, and have only just returned.

THE MOTHER: Well?

JACQUES HURY: You know, she is old and feeble.
She says she wishes to see and bless

Her daughter-in-law before she dies.

THE MOTHER: Can she not come to the wedding?

JACQUES HURY: She is ill, she cannot wait.

And this harvest time, too, when there is so
much to be done

Is not the time to be married.

We have just been talking about it, Violaine
and I, just now, very pleasantly,

And we have decided that it is best to wait till
The autumn.

Until then she will stay at Braine with my mother.

THE MOTHER: Is this your wish, Violaine?

VIOLAINE: Yes, mother.

THE MOTHER: But what! Do you wish to go away
this very day?

VIOLAINE: This very evening.

JACQUES HURY: I shall go with her.

Time is short and work pressing in this month
of hay and harvest. I have already stayed
away too long.

THE MOTHER: Stay, Violaine! Do not go away
from us, thou too!

VIOLAINE: It is only for a short time, mother!

THE MOTHER: A short time, you promise?

JACQUES HURY: A short time, and when autumn
comes

Here she will be with us again, never to go away
any more.

THE MOTHER: Ah, Jacques! Why do you let her
go away?

JACQUES HURY: Do you think it is not hard for me?

MARA: Mother, what they both say is reasonable.

THE MOTHER: It is hard to see my child leave me.

VIOLAINE: Do not be sad, mother!

What does it matter that we should wait a few
days?

It is only a little time to pass.

Am I not sure of your affection? and of Mara's? and of Jacques', my betrothed?

Is it not so, Jacques? He is mine as I am his, and nothing can separate us? Look at me, dear Jacques. See how he weeps to see me go away!

This is not the time for weeping, mother! am I not young and beautiful and loved by every-body?

My father has gone away, it is true, but he has left me the tenderest of husbands, the friend who will never forsake me.

So it is not the time to weep, but to rejoice. Ah, dear mother, how beautiful life is, and how happy I am!

MARA: And you, Jacques, what do you say? You do not look very happy.

JACQUES HURY: Is it not natural that I should be sad?

MARA: Come! it is only a separation for a few months!

JACQUES HURY: Too long for my heart.

MARA: Listen, Violaine, how well he said that! And how is this, my sister, you so sad too? Smile at me with that charming mouth! Raise those blue eyes that our father loved so much. See Jacques! Look at your wife and see how beautiful she is when she smiles!

She will not be taken away from you! who would
be sad who has a little sun like this to shine
in his home?

Love her well for us, cruel man! Tell her to
be brave!

JACQUES HURY: Courage, Violaine!

You have not lost me; we are not lost to each other!

You see that I do not doubt your love; but do
you doubt mine?

Do I doubt you, Violaine? Do I not love you,
Violaine? Am I not sure of you,
Violaine!

I have talked about you to my mother, and you
may imagine how happy she will be to see you.

It is hard to leave the house of your parents.
But where you are going you will have a safe
shelter where no one can break in.

Neither your love nor your innocence, dear
Violaine, has anything to fear.

THE MOTHER: These are very loving words,

And yet there is something in them, and in what
you said to me, my child,

I don't know what — something strange which
does not please me.

MARA: I see nothing strange, mother.

THE MOTHER: Violaine! If I hurt you just now,
my child,

Forget what I said.

VIOLAINE: You have not hurt me.

THE MOTHER: Then let me embrace you.

(She opens her arms to her.

VIOLAINE: No, mother.

THE MOTHER: What?

VIOLAINE: No.

MARA: Violaine, that is wrong! Do you fear to have us touch thee? Why do you treat us thus, like lepers?

VIOLAINE: I have made a vow.

MARA: What vow?

VIOLAINE: That nobody shall touch me.

MARA: Until your return here?

(Silence. She lowers her head.

JACQUES HURY: Let her alone. You see she is troubled.

THE MOTHER: Go away for a moment.

(They move away.

Farewell, Violaine!

You will not deceive me, my child; you will not deceive the mother who bore thee.

What I have said to you is hard; but look at me, I am full of trouble, and I am old.

You — you are young, and you will forget.

My man is gone, and now here is my child turning away from me.

One's own sorrow is nothing, but the sorrow one has caused to others

86

Makes bitter the bread in the mouth.

Think of that, my sacrificed lamb, and say to yourself: Thus I have caused sorrow to no one.

I counselled thee as I thought for the best. Don't bear malice, Violaine! Save your sister. Must she be left to be ruined?

And God will be with you, who is your recompense.

That is all. You will never see my old face again. May God be with thee!

And you do not wish to kiss me, but I can at least give you my blessing, sweet, sweet Violaine!

VIOLAINE: Yes, mother! yes, mother!

> (*She kneels, and* THE MOTHER *makes the sign of the cross above her.*

JACQUES (*returning*): Come, Violaine, it is time to go.

MARA: Go and pray for us.

VIOLAINE (*calling*): I give you my dresses, Mara, and all my things!

Have no fear of them; you know that I have not touched them.

I did not go into that room.

—Ah, ah! my poor wedding-dress that was so pretty!

> (*She stretches out her arms as if to find support. All remain at a distance from her. She goes out tottering, followed by* JACQUES.

Act Three: Scene One

Chevoche. A large forest sparsely grown with lofty oaks and birches, with an undergrowth of pines, firs, and a few holly trees. A wide straight road has just been cut through the woods to the horizon. Workmen are removing the last stumps of trees and preparing the roadway. There is a camp at one side, with huts made of faggots, a pot over a camp-fire, etc. The camp lies in a sand-pit, where a few workmen are engaged in loading a cart with a fine white sand. An apprentice of Pierre de Craon, squatting among the dry gorse bushes, oversees the work. On either side of the new road stand two colossi made of faggots, with collars and smocks of white cloth, each with a red cross on its breast. A barrel forms the head of each colossus, with its edge cut into saw-teeth to simulate a crown, and a sort of face roughly painted on it in red. A long trumpet is fitted to the bunghole, and held in place by a board as if by an arm.

It is the end of the day. There is snow on the ground and in the sky.

It is Christmas Eve.

THE MAYOR OF CHEVOCHE: There. Now the King can come.

A WORKMAN: 'A can coom an' 'a likes. We've done our part well.

THE MAYOR (*looking around with satisfaction*): It's mighty beautiful! Fact is, it can hold everybody, as many as there are, men, women, and tiny children.

And to think 'twas the worst part, with all these bad weeds and these briars, and the marsh. It ain't the wise ones of Bruyères can teach us anything.

A WORKMAN: Their road has a beard, and teeth too, wi' all those stumps they's left us!

(*They laugh*

THE APPRENTICE (*pedantically, in a voice frightfully sharp and shrill*): Vox clamantis in deserto: Parate vias Domini et erunt prava in directa et aspera in vias planas.

It is true you have done your work well. I congratulate you, good people. It is like the road at Corpus Christi.

(*Pointing to the Giants*): And who, gentlemen, are these two beautiful and reverend persons?

A WORKMAN: Beant they handsome? It was fathe' Vincent, the old drunkard, thet made 'em. 'A said it's th' great King of Abyssinia an' his wife Bellotte.

THE APPRENTICE: For my part I thought they were Gog and Magog.

THE MAYOR: 'Tis the two Angels of Chevoche who come to salute the King their lord.

89

They'll be set a-fire when 'a passes.
Listen!   (*All listen.*

A WORKMAN: Oh, no, that beant him yet. We'd
hear the bells o' Bruyères a-ringin'.

ANOTHER: 'A won't be here afore midnight. 'A
supped at Fisme.

ANOTHER: 'Tis a good place to see from, here.
I shallna budge.

ANOTHER: Hast 'a eat, Perrot? I've on'y a mossel
o' bread, all froze.

THE MAYOR: Don't be afraid. The's a quarter
o' pork in the pot and some big sausages, and
the roebuck we killed,
And three ells o' blood-sausages, and apples, and
a good little keg of Marne wine.

THE APPRENTICE: I stay with you.

A WOMAN: And there's a good little Christmas for you.

THE APPRENTICE: It was on Christmas Day that
King Clovis was baptized at Rheims.

ANOTHER WOMAN: 'Tis Christmas Day that oor
King Charles comes back to get hi'self crowned.

ANOTHER: 'Tis a village girl, sent by God,
Who brings him back to his own.

ANOTHER: Jeanne, they call her!

ANOTHER: The Maid!

ANOTHER: Who was born on Twelfth Night!

ANOTHER: Who drove the English away from
Orleans when they besieged it!

ANOTHER WORKMAN: And who's goin' to drive 'em out of France too, all of 'em! Amen:

ANOTHER WORKMAN (*humming*): Noel! Cock-a-doodle-do! Noel! Noel come again! Rrr! how cauld it be!

> (*He wraps himself closer in his cloak.*

A WOMAN: Mus' look well t' see if the's a little man all in red clothes by th' King. That's her.

ANOTHER WOMAN: On a tall black horse.

THE FIRST WOMAN: On'y six months agone her was keepin' her father's cows.

ANOTHER WOMAN: And now her carries a banner where Jesus is in writin'.

A WORKMAN: An' that the English run away before like mice.

ANOTHER WORKMAN: Let the wicked Bourguignons o' Saponay beware!

ANOTHER WORKMAN: They'll all be at Rheims at the break o' day.

ANOTHER WORKMAN: What be they doin', those down there?

THE APPRENTICE: The two bells of the Cathedral, Baudon and Baude, will be rung at the Gloria at midnight, and they will never stop swinging and clanging until the French come.

Everybody will keep a lighted candle in his house until morning.

They expect the King to be there for the Mass
at dawn, which is "Lux fulgebit."

All the clergy will go out to meet him, three
hundred priests and the Archbishop in copes of
gold, and the monks, the Mayor and the vestry.

All that will be very beautiful on the snow, in
the bright merry sunshine, with all the people
singing "Noel"!

And they say that the King intends to get down
from his horse, and enter his good city riding
upon an ass, like our Lord.

THE MAYOR: How comes it that you did not stay
down there?

THE APPRENTICE: Master Pierre de Craon sent me
here to get sand.

THE MAYOR: What! He busies himself about sand
at such a time?

THE APPRENTICE: He says there is not much time.

THE MAYOR: But how could he employ himself better than in making this road, as we do?

THE APPRENTICE: He says that his work is not to
make roads for the King, but a dwelling for
God.

THE MAYOR: Of what use would Rheims be if
the King could not reach it?

THE APPRENTICE: But what use would the road be
if there is no church at the end of it?

THE MAYOR: He is not a good Frenchman.

THE APPRENTICE: He says that he knows nothing but his work. If anybody talks politics to us, we blacken his nose with the bottom of the frying-pan.

THE MAYOR: He has not even been able to finish his Justice, though 'tis ten years they've been working on it.

THE APPRENTICE: On the contrary! All the stone is polished, and the woodwork is in place; it's only the spire that has not yet done growing.

THE MAYOR: They never work on it.

THE APPRENTICE: The master is preparing the glass for his windows now, and that is why he sends us here for sand;

Though that is not his craft.

All winter he has worked among his furnaces.

To make light, my poor people, is more difficult than to make gold,

To breathe on this heavy matter and make it transparent, "according as our bodies of mud shall be changed into bodies of glory,"

As Saint Paul said.

And he says that he must find for each colour

The mother-colour itself, just as God himself made it.

That is why, into his great clean vessels, full of shining water, he pours jacinth, ultramarine, rich gold, vermilion,

And he watches these beautiful rose-coloured
liquids to see what happens to them in the
sunshine, and by virtue of the grace of God,
and how they mingle and bloom in the matrass.
And he says there is not one colour which he
cannot make out of his own knowledge alone,
As his body makes red and blue.
Because he wishes the Justice of Rheims to shine
like the morning on the day of her nuptials.

THE MAYOR: They say he has leprosy.

THE APPRENTICE: That is not true! I saw him
naked last summer.
While he bathed in the Aisne at Soissons. I
know what I say!
His flesh is as healthy as a child's.

THE MAYOR: It is queer, all the same. Why
did he keep himself hidden so long?

THE APPRENTICE: That is a lie.

THE MAYOR: I know, I am older than you. You
mustn't get angry, little man. It doesn't matter
if he be sick in the body.
It isn't with his body he works.

THE APPRENTICE: Better not let him hear you say
that! I remember how he punished one of us because he stayed all the time in his corner, drawing:
He sent him up on the scaffolding to serve the
masons all day and pass them their hods and
their stones,

Saying that by the end of the day he would know
two things better than he could learn them by
rule and design: the weight a man can carry
and the height of his body.

And as the grace of God multiplies each of our
good deeds,

So he taught us about what he calls "the shekel
of the Temple," and this dwelling of God of
which each man who does all that his body
is capable of doing is like a secret foundation;

What means the thumb, and the hand, and the
arm's length, and the spread of both our arms,
and the arm extended, and the circle it makes,

And the foot and the step;

And how all these things are never the same.

Do you think Father Noah was indifferent to
the body when he built the ark? and are these
things of no account:

The number of paces from the door to the altar,
and the height the eye may be lifted to, and
the number of souls the two sides of the Church
may hold all at the same time?

For the heathen artist made everything from the
outside, but we make all from within, like the bees,

And as the soul does for the body: nothing is
lifeless, everything lives,

Everything gives thanks in action.

THE MAYOR: The little man talks well.

A Workman: Hear him, like a magpie, all full of his master's words.

The Apprentice: Speak with respect of Pierre de Craon!

The Mayor: 'Tis true he's a burgher of Rheims, and they call him Master of the Compass.
As they used to call Messire Loys
The Master of the Rule.

Another: Throw some wood on the fire,
Perrot, look it's beginning to snow.

> (*It snows. Night has come. Enter* MARA *dressed in black, carrying a bundle under her cloak.*)

Mara: Are these the people of Chevoche?

The Mayor: 'Tis ourselves.

Mara: Praised be Jesus Christ.

The Mayor: Amen!

Mara: Is it around here I'll find the little cell of the Géyn?

The Mayor: Where the leper woman lives?

Mara: Yes.

The Mayor: Not exactly here, but close by.

Another: You want to see the leper woman?

Mara: Yes.

A Man: She can't be seen; she always wears a veil over her face, as it's ordered.

Another: And well ordered! it isn't myself as wants to see her.

Mara: It's a long time you've had her?

A Man: A'most eight years, and we'd like it well not to have her at all.

Mara: Is that because she has done harm?

A Man: No, but all t'same it's unlucky to have these varmint kind of folk near by.

The Mayor: And then, 'tis the parish that feeds her.

A Man: By the way, I bet they've forgot to take her her bite to eat for three days, with all these doings about the road!

A Woman: And what do you want o' this woman?
> (Mara *makes no reply, but stands, looking at the fire.*

A Woman: A person would say it's a child you're a-holdin' in your arms?

Another Woman: It's a fearsome cold to take out little children at such an hour.

Mara: It is not cold.
> (*Silence. There is heard, from the darkness under the trees, the sound of a wooden rattle.*

An Old Woman: Wait! there's her! there's her click-click! Holy Virgin! what a pity her ain't dead!

A Woman: 'A comes to ask for her food. No fear her'll forget that!

A Man: What a plague 'tis to feed such varmint.

Another: Toss her somethin'. She mustn't come

anigh to us. First thing you know she'd give us the poison.

ANOTHER: No meat, Perrot! It's fast day, it's Christmas Eve! *(They laugh.*

Throw her this mossel o' bread that's froze. Good enough for the like o' her!

A MAN *(calling)*: Heigh, No-face! Heigh, Jeanne, I say, hallo, rotting one!

(The black form of the leper woman is seen on the snow. MARA *looks at her.*

Catch it!

(He throws her swiftly a piece of bread. She stoops and picks it up and goes away. MARA *follows her.*

A MAN: Where is it she's going?

ANOTHER: Here, woman! hallo! where be you going, what be you doing?

*(*MARA *and* THE WOMAN *go farther away.*

Act Three: Scene Two

They disappear within the forest, leaving their tracks upon the snow. The night brightens. The brilliant moon, surrounded by an immense halo, lights up a hillock covered with heather and white sand. Enormous sandstone rocks, fantastically formed, rise here and there like beasts belonging to the fossil ages, like inexplicable monuments or idols with deformed heads and limbs. And the leper woman conducts MARA *to the cave where she lives, a kind of low cavern in which it is impossible to stand upright. The back of the cave is closed, leaving only an opening for the smoke.*

Act Three: Scene Three

VIOLAINE: Who is this
That does not fear to walk with the leper woman?
You must know that it is dangerous to be near
her, and her breath is deadly.

MARA: It is I, Violaine.

VIOLAINE: O voice, so long unheard! Is it you,
mother?

MARA: It is I, Violaine.

VIOLAINE: It is your voice and another.
Let me light this fire, for it is very cold. And
this torch, too.

> (*She lights a fire of turf and heather by means
> of live embers which she takes from a pot,
> and then the torch.*

MARA: It is I, Violaine; Mara, your sister.

VIOLAINE: Dear sister, hail! How good of you to
come! But do you not fear me?

MARA: I fear nothing in this world.

VIOLAINE: How much your voice has become like
Maman's!

MARA: Violaine, our dear mother is no more.

> (*Silence.*

VIOLAINE: When did she die?

MARA: In that same month after your departure.

VIOLAINE: Knowing nothing?

MARA: I do not know.

VIOLAINE: Poor *Maman!*
May God have thy soul in his keeping!

MARA: And our father has not yet come back.

VIOLAINE: And you two?

MARA: It is well with us.

VIOLAINE: Everything at home is as you wish it?

MARA: Everything is well.

VIOLAINE: I know it could not be otherwise
With Jacques and you.

MARA: You should see what we have done! We have three more ploughs.
You would not recognize Combernon.
And we are going to pull down those old walls,
Now that the King has come back.

VIOLAINE: And are you happy together, Mara?

MARA: Yes. We are happy. He loves me
As I love him.

VIOLAINE: God be praised.

MARA: Violaine!
You do not see what I hold in my arms?

VIOLAINE: I cannot see.

MARA: Lift your veil, then.

VIOLAINE: Under that I have another.

MARA: You cannot see any more?

VIOLAINE: I have no longer any eyes.
The soul lives alone in the ruined body.

MARA: Blind!
How then are you able to walk so straight?

VIOLAINE: I hear.

MARA: What do you hear?

VIOLAINE: I hear all things exist with me.

MARA (*significantly*): And I, Violaine, do you hear me?

VIOLAINE: God has given me the same intelligence Which He has given to us all.

MARA: Do you hear me, Violaine?

VIOLAINE: Ah, poor Mara!

MARA: Do you hear me, Violaine?

VIOLAINE: What would you have of me, dear sister?

MARA: To join you in praise of this God who has struck you with the pestilence.

VIOLAINE: Then let us praise Him, on this Eve of His Nativity.

MARA: It is easy to be a saint when leprosy helps us.

VIOLAINE: I do not know, not being one.

MARA: We must turn to God when everything else is gone.

VIOLAINE: He at least will not fail us.

MARA (*softly*): Perhaps, who knows, Violaine, tell me?

VIOLAINE: Life fails, but not the death where I now live.

MARA: Heretic! are you sure, then, of your salvation?

VIOLAINE: I am sure of the goodness of Him who has provided for everything.

MARA: We see His first instalment.

VIOLAINE: I have faith in God who has ordained my destiny.

MARA: What do you know of Him who is invisible, who is never manifest?

VIOLAINE: He is not more invisible to me now than all the rest.

MARA (*ironically*): He is with you, little dove, and He loves you!

VIOLAINE: As with all who are wretched, Himself with me.

MARA: Surely how very great is His love!

VIOLAINE: As the love of the fire for the wood it flames above.

MARA: He has cruelly punished you.

VIOLAINE: Not more that it was due to me.

MARA: And already, he to whom you had submitted your body has forgotten you?

VIOLAINE: I have not submitted my body!

MARA: Sweet Violaine! lying Violaine! Did I not see you tenderly kiss Pierre de Craon the morning of that beautiful day in June?

VIOLAINE: You saw all, and there was nothing else.

MARA: Why, then, did you kiss him so feelingly?

VIOLAINE: The poor man was a leper, and I, I was so happy that day!

MARA: In all innocence, wasn't it?

VIOLAINE: Like a little girl who kisses a poor little boy.

MARA: Ought I to believe that, Violaine?

VIOLAINE: It is true.

MARA: Don't say, too, that it was of your own will you abandoned Jacques to me?

VIOLAINE: No, not of my own will. I loved him! I am not so good as that.

MARA: Ought he to have loved you the same, though you were a leper?

VIOLAINE: I did not expect it.

MARA: Who would love a leper woman?

VIOLAINE: My heart is pure!

MARA: But what did Jacques know of that? He believes you guilty.

VIOLAINE: Our mother had told me that you loved him.

MARA: Don't say it was she who made you a leper.

VIOLAINE: God in His goodness warned me.

MARA: So that when our mother spoke to you . . .

VIOLAINE: It was His voice that I heard.

MARA: But why allow yourself to seem guilty?

VIOLAINE: Should I have done nothing, then, on my part?
Poor Jacquin! Was it necessary to leave him still regretting me?

MARA: Say that you did not love him at all.

VIOLAINE: I did not love him, Mara.

MARA: But I would never have let him go like that.

VIOLAINE: Was it I who let him go?

MARA: It would have killed me.

VIOLAINE: And am I living?

MARA: Now I am happy with him.

VIOLAINE: Peace be unto you!

MARA: And I have given him a child, Violaine! a dear little girl. A sweet little girl.

VIOLAINE: Peace be unto you!

MARA: Our happiness is great. But yours is greater, with God.

VIOLAINE: And I too knew what happiness was eight years ago, and my heart was ravished with it.

So much, that I madly asked God — ah! — that it might last for ever!

And God heard me in a strange manner! Will my leprosy ever be cured? No, no, as long as there remains a particle of my flesh to be devoured.

Will the love in my heart be cured? Never, as long as my immortal soul lives to nourish it.

Does your husband understand you, Mara?

MARA: What man understands a woman?

VIOLAINE: Happy is she who can be known, heart and soul, who can give herself utterly.

Jacques — what would he have done with all that
I could have given him?

MARA: You have transferred your faith to Another?

VIOLAINE: Love has ended in pain, and pain has
ended in love.

The wood we set on fire gives not only ashes, but
a flame as well.

MARA: But of what use is this blind fire that gives
to others

Neither light nor heat?

VIOLAINE: Is it not something that it does me
service?

Do not begrudge to a creature consumed,

Afflicted to the uttermost depths, this light that
illumines her within!

And if you could pass but one night only in my skin,
you would not say that this fire gives no heat.

Man is the priest, but it is not forbidden to woman
to be victim.

God is miserly, and does not permit any creature
to be set on fire

Unless some impurity be burned with him,

His own, or that which surrounds him, as when
the living embers in the censer are stirred.

And truly these are unhappy times.

The people have no father. They look around,
and they know no longer where the King is,
or the Pope.

That is why my body agonizes here for all
Christendom which is perishing.

Powerful is suffering when it is as voluntary as
sin!

You saw me kiss that leper, Mara?

Ah, the chalice of sorrow is deep,

And who once sets his lip to it can never withdraw it again of his own free will.

MARA: Take my sorrow upon thee, too!

VIOLAINE: I have already taken it.

MARA: Violaine! if there is still something living,
that was once my sister, under that veil and
in that ruined body,

Remember that we were children together! Have
pity upon me!

VIOLAINE: Speak, dear sister. Have faith! Tell
me all!

MARA: Violaine, I am a wretched woman, and my
pain is greater than yours!

VIOLAINE: Greater, sister?

  (MARA, *with a loud cry, opens her cloak and
lifts up the corpse of a baby.*

Look! Take it!

VIOLAINE: What is this?

MARA: Look, I tell you! take it! Take it, I give
it to you.   (*She lays the corpse in her arms.*

VIOLAINE: Ah! I feel a rigid little body! a poor
little cold face!

MARA: Ha! ha! Violaine! My child! my little girl!
That is her sweet little face! that is her poor
little body!

VIOLAINE (*speaking low*): Dead, Mara?

MARA: Take her, I give her to you!

VIOLAINE: Peace, Mara!

MARA: They wanted to take her away from me.
but I would not let them! and I ran away
with her.

But you, take her, Violaine. Here, take her;
you see, I give her to you.

VIOLAINE: What do you wish me to do, Mara?

MARA: What do I wish you to do? do you not
understand?

I tell you she is dead! I tell you she is dead!

VIOLAINE: Her soul lives with God. She follows
the Lamb. She is with all the blessèd little
girls.

MARA: But for me she is dead!

VIOLAINE: You readily give me her body! give the
rest to God.

MARA: No! no! no! You shall never trick me
with your nunnish rigmaroles! No, I shall
never be silenced.

This milk that burns my breast cries out to God
like the blood of Abel!

Have I got fifty children to tear out of my body?
have I got fifty souls to tear out of my soul?

Do you know what it is to be rent in two in order to bring into the world this little wailing creature?

And the midwife told me I should have no more children.

But if I had a hundred children it would not be my little Aubaine.

VIOLAINE: Accept, submit.

MARA: Violaine, you know well I have a hard head. I am one who never gives up, and who accepts nothing.

VIOLAINE: Poor sister!

MARA: Violaine, they are so sweet, these little ones, and it hurts you so when this cruel little mouth bites your breast!

VIOLAINE (*caressing the face*): How cold her little face is!

MARA (*speaking low*): He knows nothing yet.

VIOLAINE (*also speaking low*): He was not home?

MARA: He has gone to Rheims to sell his grain. She died suddenly, in two hours.

VIOLAINE: Whom was she like?

MARA: Like him, Violaine. She is not only mine, she is his, too. Only her eyes are like mine.

VIOLAINE: Poor Jacquin!

MARA: It was not to hear you say poor Jacquin! that I came here.

VIOLAINE: What do you wish of me, then?

MARA: Violaine, do you want to know? Tell me, do you know what a soul is that damns itself, Of its own will, to all eternity?

Do you know what it is in the heart that really blasphemes?

There is a devil who, while I was running, sang me a little song,

Do you wish to hear the things he taught me?

VIOLAINE: Do not say these horrible things!

MARA: Then give me back my child that I gave you.

VIOLAINE: You gave me only a corpse.

MARA: And you, give it back to me alive!

VIOLAINE: Mara, what do you dare to say?

MARA: I will not have it that my child is dead.

VIOLAINE: Is it in my power to bring the dead to life?

MARA: I don't know, I have only you to help me.

VIOLAINE: Is it in my power to bring the dead to life, like God?

MARA: Of what use are you, then?

VIOLAINE: To suffer and to supplicate!

MARA: But of what use is it to suffer and supplicate if you give me not back my child?

VIOLAINE: God knows. It is enough for Him that I serve Him.

MARA: But I — I am deaf, and I do not hear! and I cry to you from the depths where I am fallen! Violaine! Violaine!

Give me back that child I gave you! See! I
give in, I humiliate myself! have pity on me!
Have pity on me, Violaine, and give me back
that child you took from me.

VIOLAINE: Only He who took it can give it
back!

MARA: Give it back to me then! Ah, I know
it is all your fault.

VIOLAINE: My fault!

MARA: Then let it not be yours.
It is mine, forgive me!
But give her back to me, my sister!

VIOLAINE: But you see it is dead.

MARA: You lie! it is not dead! Ah! figure-of-tow,
ah, heart-of-a-sheep! Ah, if I had access to
your God as you have,
He would not take my little ones away from me
so easily!

VIOLAINE: Ask me to re-create heaven and earth!

MARA: But it is written that you may blow on
that mountain and cast it into the sea.

VIOLAINE: I can, if I am a saint.

MARA: You must be a saint when a wretched being
prays to you.

VIOLAINE: Ah, supreme temptation!
I swear, and I declare, and I protest before God
that I am not a saint!

MARA: Then give me back my child.

VIOLAINE: O my God, you see into my heart.

I swear and I protest before God that I am not a saint!

MARA: Violaine, give me back my child!

VIOLAINE: Why will you not leave me in peace? Why do you come thus to torment me in my tomb?

Am I of any worth? do I influence God? am I like God?

It is God himself you are asking me to judge.

MARA: I ask you only for my child. (*Pause.*

VIOLAINE (*raising her finger*): Listen.

(*Silence. A distant, almost imperceptible, sound of bells.*

MARA: I hear nothing.

VIOLAINE: The Christmas bells, the bells announcing the midnight Mass!

O Mara, a little child is born to us!

MARA: Then give me back mine.

(*Trumpets in the distance.*

VIOLAINE: What is that?

MARA: It is the King going to Rheims. Have you not heard of the road the peasants have cut through the forest?

And they can keep all the wood they cut.

It is a little shepherdess who guides the King through the middle of France

To Rheims, to be crowned there.

VIOLAINE: Praised be God, who does all these wonderful things!

> (*Again the sound of bells, very distinct.*

MARA: How loud the bells ring for the *Gloria!* The wind blows this way.

They are ringing in three villages all at once.

VIOLAINE: Let us pray, with all the universe! Thou art not cold, Mara?

MARA: I am cold only in my heart.

VIOLAINE: Let us pray. It is long since we celebrated Christmas together.

Fear nothing. I have taken your grief upon myself. Look! and that which you have given me lies close against my heart.

Do not weep! This is not the time to weep, when the salvation of all mankind is already born. *(Bells in the distance, less clear.*

MARA: The snow has stopped, and the stars are shining.

VIOLAINE: Look! Do you see this Book?

The priest who visits me now and then left it with me.

MARA: I see it.

VIOLAINE: Take it, will you? and read me the Christmas Service, the First Lesson of each of the three Nocturnes.

> (MARA *takes the Book and reads.*

THE TIDINGS BROUGHT TO MARY

1 Nevertheless, the dimness shall not be such as was in her vexation, when at the first he lightly afflicted the land of Zebulun and the land of Naphtali, and afterward did more grievously afflict her by the way of the sea, beyond Jordan, in Galilee of the nations.

2 The people that walked in darkness have seen a great light: they that dwell in the land of the shadow of death, upon them hath the light shined.

3 Thou hast multiplied the nation, and not increased the joy: they joy before thee according to the joy in harvest, and as men rejoice when they divide the spoil.

4 For thou hast broken the yoke of his burden; and the staff of his shoulder, the rod of his oppressor, as in the day of Midian.

5 For every battle of the warrior is with confused noise, and garments rolled in blood; but this shall be with burning and fuel of fire.

6 For unto us a child is born, unto us a son is given, and the government shall be upon his shoulder; and his name shall be called Wonderful, Counsellor, The mighty God, The everlasting Father, the Prince of Peace.

[1] Isaiah ix, 1–6.

VIOLAINE (*raising her face*): Listen!   (*Silence.*

VOICES OF ANGELS in heaven, heard only by Violaine:

CHOIR:[1] HODIE NOBIS DE CÆLO PAX VERA DE-
SCENDIT, HODIE PER TOTUM MUNDUM MELLI-
FLUI FACTI SUNT CÆLI.

A VOICE:[2] HODIE ILLUXIT NOBIS DIES REDEMP-
TIONIS NOVÆ, REPARATIONIS ANTIQUÆ, FELICI-
TATIS ÆTERNÆ.

CHOIR: HODIE PER TOTUM MUNDUM MELLIFLUI
FACTI SUNT CÆLI.

(VIOLAINE *lifts her finger in warning.*
Silence. MARA *listens and looks uneasily.*

MARA: I hear nothing.

VIOLAINE: Read on, Mara.

MARA (*continuing to read*):

SERMON OF SAINT LEO, POPE

Our Saviour, dearly beloved, was to-day born:
let us rejoice. For there should be no loop-
hole open to sorrow on the birthday of Life,
which, the fear of Death being at last consumed, filleth us with the joy of eternity promised. No one from this gladness is excluded,
as one and the same cause for happiness exists
for us all: for Our Lord, the destroyer of sin

---

[1] The voices are like those of heroic young men singing solemnly in unison,
with retarded movement and very simple cadence at the end of phrases.
[2] Like the voice of a child.

and Death, having found no one exempt from
sin, came to deliver every one. Let the sinless
exult insomuch as his palm is at hand; let the
sinful rejoice . . .

> (*Suddenly a brilliant and prolonged sound of
> trumpets very near. Shouts resound
> through the forest.*

MARA: The King! The King of France!

> (*Again and again the blare of the trumpets,
> unutterably piercing, solemn, and tri-
> umphant.*

MARA (*in a low voice*): The King of France who
goes to Rheims! (*Silence.*

Violaine! (*Silence.*

Do you hear me, Violaine?

> (*Silence. She goes on with the reading.*

. . . Let the sinful rejoice insomuch as forgive-
ness is offered to him. Let the Gentile be of
good cheer, because he is bidden to share life.
For the Son of God, according to the fulness
of this time which the inscrutable depth of the
Divine counsel hath disposed, took on Himself
the nature of mankind so that He might recon-
cile it to its maker, and that this deviser of
Death, Satan, by that which he had vanquished
might be in his turn conquered.

VOICES OF ANGELS (*heard only by* VIOLAINE, *as
before*):

CHOIR: O MAGNUM MYSTERIUM ET ADMIRABILE SACRAMENTUM UT ANIMALIA VIDERINT DOMINUM NATUM JACENTEM IN PRÆSEPIO! BEATA VIRGO CUJUS VISCERA MERUERUNT PORTARE DOMINUM CHRISTUM.

A VOICE: AVE, MARIA, GRATIA PLENA, DOMINUS TECUM.

CHOIR: BEATA VIRGO CUJUS VISCERA MERUERUNT PORTARE DOMINUM CHRISTUM.   (*Pause.*

MARA: Violaine, I am not worthy to read this Book! Violaine, I know that my heart is too hard, and I am sorry for it: I wish I could be different.

VIOLAINE: Read on, Mara. You do not know who chants the responses.   (*Silence.*

MARA (*with an effort takes up the Book, and reads in a trembling voice*):

The Holy Gospel according to Saint Luke.[1]

(*They both stand up.*

1 And it came to pass in those days, that there went out a decree from Cæsar Augustus, that all the world should be taxed. (And the rest.)

(*They sit down.*

HOMILY OF SAINT GREGORY, POPE
(*She stops, overcome by emotion. — The trumpets sound a last time in the distance.*

MARA:

Forasmuch as, by the grace of God, we are this

[1] Luke ii, 1.

117

day thrice to celebrate the solemnities of Mass, we may not speak at length on the gospel that hath just been read. However, the birth of our Redeemer bids us address you at least in a few words. Wherefore, at the time of this birth, should there have been a census of all the people except clearly to manifest that He who was appearing in the flesh just then was numbering his Elect for eternity? On the contrary, the Prophet saith of the wicked: they shall be deleted from the Book of the Living and they shall not be written down among the Righteous. It is meet also that He should be born in Bethlehem. For Bethlehem means the House of Bread, and Jesus Christ saith of Himself: I am the Living Bread descended from Heaven. Therefore had the place in which our Lord was born been called the House of Bread in order that He who was to feed our hearts with internal satiety should there appear in the substance of flesh. He was born, not in the house of his parents, but by the roadside, no doubt to show that by taking on humanity He was being born in a place strange to Him.

VOICES OF ANGELS:

CHOIR: BEATA VISCERA MARIÆ VIRGINIS QUÆ PORTAVERUNT ÆTERNI PATRIS FILIUM; ET BEATA UBERA QUÆ LACTAVERUNT CHRISTUM DOMINUM.

QUI HODIE PRO SALUTE MUNDI DE VIRGINE NASCI
DIGNATUS EST.

A VOICE: DIES SANCTIFICATUS ILLUXIT NOBIS;
VENITE, GENTES, ET ADORATE DOMINUM.

CHOIR: QUI HODIE PRO SALUTE MUNDI DE VIRGINE
NASCI DIGNATUS EST. (*Long silence.*

VOICES OF ANGELS (*again, almost imperceptible*):

CHOIR: VERBUM CARO FACTUM EST ET HABI-
TAVIT IN NOBIS: ET VIDIMUS GLORIAM EJUS,
GLORIAM QUASI UNIGENITI A PATRE, PLENUM
GRATIÆ ET VERITATIS

A VOICE: OMNIA PER IPSUM FACTA SUNT ET SINE
IPSO FACTUM EST NIHIL.

CHOIR: ET VIDIMUS GLORIAM EJUS, GLORIAM QUASI
UNIGENITI A PATRE, PLENUM GRATIÆ ET VERI-
TATIS.

A VOICE: GLORIA PATRI ET FILIO ET SPIRITUI
SANCTO.

CHOIR: ET VIDIMUS GLORIAM EJUS, GLORIAM QUASI
UNIGENITI A PATRE, PLENUM GRATIÆ ET VERI-
TATIS. (*Long silence.*

VIOLAINE (*suddenly cries out in a stifled voice*): Ah!

MARA: What is it?

> (*With her hand she makes her a sign to be
> silent. — Silence. — The first flush of dawn
> appears.*

> (VIOLAINE *puts her hand under her cloak as
> if to fasten her dress again.*

MARA: Violaine, I see something moving under your cloak!

VIOLAINE (*as if she were awakening little by little*): Is it you, Mara? good morning, sister. I feel the breath of the new-born day on my face.

MARA: Violaine! Violaine! is it your arm that stirs? Again I see something moving.

VIOLAINE: Peace, Mara, it is Christmas Day, when all joy is born!

MARA: What joy is there for me unless my child lives?

VIOLAINE: And for us, too — a little child is born to us!

MARA: In the name of the living God, what say you?

VIOLAINE: "Behold, I bring thee glad tidings . . ."

MARA: Your cloak — it moves again!

(*The little bare foot of a baby, moving lazily, appears in the opening of the cloak.*

VIOLAINE: ". . . Because a man has appeared in the world!"

(MARA *falls upon her knees, with a deep sigh, her forehead on the knees of her sister.* VIOLAINE *caresses her.*

VIOLAINE: Poor sister! she weeps. She, too, has had too much sorrow.

(*Silence.* VIOLAINE *kisses her head.*

Take it, Mara! Would you leave the child
always with me?

MARA (*she takes the child from under the cloak and
looks at it wildly*): It lives!

VIOLAINE (*she walks out of the cave a few steps upon
the heather. By the first light of the bitter cold
morning can be seen, first, the pine and birch
trees hoary with frost, then, at the end of an
immense snow-covered plain, seeming very small
on the top of its hill, but clearly etched in the pure
air, the five-towered silhouette of Monsanvierge*):
Glory to God!

MARA: It lives!

VIOLAINE: Peace on earth to men!

MARA: It lives! it lives!

VIOLAINE: It lives and we live.

And the face of the Father appeared on the
earth born again and comforted.

MARA: My child lives!

VIOLAINE (*raising her finger*): Listen! (*Silence.*
I hear the Angelus ringing at Monsanvierge.
     (*She crosses herself and prays. The child
     awakes.*

MARA (*whispering*): It is I, Aubaine; dost know
me?   (*The child moves about and whines.*
What is it, my joy? What is it, my treasure?
     (*The child opens its eyes, looks at its mother
     and begins to cry. MARA looks closely at it.*

Violaine!
What does this mean? Its eyes were black,
And now they are blue like yours.   (*Silence.*
Ah!
And what is this drop of milk I see on its lips?

Act Four: Scene One

Night. The large kitchen, as in Act I, *empty.
A lamp is on the table. The outer door is half open.*

Mara *enters from without, and carefully closes the
door. She stands still for a moment in the centre of the
room, looking toward the door, and listening.*

*Then she takes the lamp and goes out by another door
without making any sound.*

*The stage remains dark. Nothing can be seen but
the fire of some live coals on the hearth.*

Act Four: Scene Two

Two or three blasts of a horn are heard in the dis-
tance. Sounds of calling. Movement in the farm.
Then the noise of opening doors, and the grinding of
approaching cart-wheels. Loud knocks at the door.
VOICE FROM WITHOUT (*calling*): Hallo!

       (*Noise in the upper story of a window opening.*
VOICE OF JACQUES HURY: Who is there?

VOICE FROM WITHOUT: Open the door!

VOICE OF JACQUES HURY: What do you want?

VOICE FROM WITHOUT: Open the door!

VOICE OF JACQUES HURY: Who are you?

VOICE FROM WITHOUT: Open the door so that I
  can tell you!   (*Pause.*

      (JACQUES HURY, *with a candle in his hand,*
        enters the room; he opens the door. After
        a slight pause,

    Enter PIERRE DE CRAON, *carrying the body*
      of a woman wrapped up in his arms. He
      lays his burden very carefully upon the
      table. Then he lifts his head. The two
      men stare at each other in the candlelight.

PIERRE DE CRAON: Jacques Hury, do you not
  recognize me?

JACQUES HURY: Pierre de Craon?

PIERRE DE CRAON: It is I.

> (*They continue to look at each other.*

JACQUES HURY: And what is this you bring me?

PIERRE DE CRAON: I found her half-buried in my sandpit, there where I seek what I need
For my glass ovens, and for the mortar —
Half-hidden under a great cart-load of sand, under a cart standing on end from which they had taken off the backboard.
She is still alive. It is I who took it upon myself to bring her to you
Here.

JACQUES HURY: Why here?

PIERRE DE CRAON: That at least she might die under her father's roof!

JACQUES HURY: There is no roof here but mine.

PIERRE DE CRAON: Jacques, here is Violaine.

JACQUES HURY: I know no Violaine.

PIERRE DE CRAON: Have you never heard of the Leper Woman of Chevoche?

JACQUES HURY: What does that matter to me? You lepers, it is for you to scrape each other's sores.

PIERRE DE CRAON: I am not a leper any more; I was cured long ago.

JACQUES HURY: Cured?

PIERRE DE CRAON: Year after year the disease grew less, and I am now healthy.

JACQUES HURY: And this one, she too will be cured presently.

PIERRE DE CRAON: You are more leprous than she and I.

JACQUES HURY: But I don't ask to be taken out of my hole in the sand.

PIERRE DE CRAON: And even if she had been guilty, you ought to remember.

JACQUES HURY: Is it true that she kissed you on the mouth?

PIERRE DE CRAON (*looking at him*): It is true, poor child!

JACQUES HURY: She moves, she is coming to herself.

PIERRE DE CRAON: I leave you with her.

(*He goes out.*

Act Four: Scene Three

(JACQUES HURY *sits down near the table and looks silently at* VIOLAINE.

VIOLAINE (*coming to herself and stretching forth her hand*): Where am I, and who is there?

JACQUES HURY: At Monsanvierge, and it is I who am near you. (*Pause.*

VIOLAINE (*speaking as she used to do*): Good morning, Jacques. (*Silence.*

Jacques, you still care for me, then?

JACQUES HURY: The wound is not healed.

VIOLAINE: Poor boy!

And I, too, have I not suffered a little too?

JACQUES HURY: What possessed you to kiss that leper on the mouth!

VIOLAINE: Jacques! you must reproach me quickly with all you have in your heart against me, that we may finish with all that.

For we have other things still to say.

And I want to hear you say just once again those words I loved so much: *Dear Violaine! Sweet Violaine!*

For the time that remains to us is short.

JACQUES HURY: I have nothing more to say to you.

VIOLAINE: Come here, cruel man!

> (*He approaches her, where she lies.*

Come nearer to me.

> (*She takes his hand and draws him to her.*
> *He kneels awkwardly at her side.*

Jacques, you must believe me. I swear it before
God, who is looking upon us!

I was never guilty with Pierre de Craon.

JACQUES HURY: Why, then, did you kiss him?

VIOLAINE: Ah, he was so sad and I was so happy.

JACQUES HURY: I don't believe you.

> (*She lays her hand a moment on his head.*

VIOLAINE: Do you believe me now?

> (*He hides his face in her dress and sobs*
> *heavily.*

JACQUES HURY: Ah, Violaine! cruel Violaine!

VIOLAINE: Not cruel, but sweet, sweet Violaine!

JACQUES HURY: It is true, then? yes, it was only
I you loved?

> (*Silence.   She gives him her other hand.*

VIOLAINE: Jacques, no doubt it was all too beautiful, and we should have been too happy.

JACQUES HURY: You have cruelly deceived me.

VIOLAINE: Deceived? this silver flower on my side
did not lie.

JACQUES HURY: What was I to believe, Violaine?

VIOLAINE: If you had believed in me,
Who knows but what you might have cured me?

JACQUES HURY: Was I not to believe my own eyes?

VIOLAINE: That is true. You ought to have believed your own eyes, that is right.

One does not marry a leper. One does not marry an unfaithful woman.

Do not regret anything, Jacques. There, it is better as it is.

JACQUES HURY: Did you know that Mara loved me?

VIOLAINE: I knew it. My mother herself had told me.

JACQUES HURY: Thus everything was in league with her against me!

VIOLAINE: Jacques, there is already enough sorrow in the world.

It is best not to be willingly the cause of a great sorrow to others.

JACQUES HURY: But what of my sorrow?

VIOLAINE: That is another thing, Jacques. Are you not happy to be with me?

JACQUES: Yes, Violaine.

VIOLAINE: Where I am, there is patience, not sorrow.   (*Silence.*

The world's grief is great.

It is too hard to suffer, and not to know why.

But that which others do not know, I have learned, and thou must share my knowledge.

Jacques, have we not been separated long enough now? should we let any barrier remain between us? Must it still be that death shall separate us?

Only that which is ill should perish, and that which should not perish is that which suffers.

Happy is he who suffers, and who knows why. Now my task is finished.

JACQUES HURY: And mine begins.

VIOLAINE: What! do you find the cup where I have drunk so bitter?

JACQUES HURY: And now I have lost you for ever!

VIOLAINE: Tell me, why lost?

JACQUES HURY: You are dying.

VIOLAINE: Jacques, you must understand me! Of what use is the finest perfume in a sealed vase? it serves for nothing.

JACQUES HURY: No, Violaine.

VIOLAINE: Of what use has my body been to me, having hidden away my heart so that you could not see it, but you saw only the scar on the outside of the worthless shell.

JACQUES HURY: I was hard and blind!

VIOLAINE: Now I am broken utterly, and the perfume is set free.

And Behold, you believe everything, simply because I laid my hand on your head.

JACQUES HURY: I believe. I do not doubt any
more.

VIOLAINE: And tell me, where is the Justice in
all that, this justice you spoke of so proudly?

JACQUES HURY: I am no longer proud.

VIOLAINE: Come, leave Justice alone. It is not
for us to call her and to make her come.

JACQUES HURY: Violaine, how you have suffered
in these eight long years!

VIOLAINE: But not in vain. Many things are
consumed in the flame of a heart that burns.

JACQUES HURY: Deliverance is near.

VIOLAINE: Blessed be the hand that led me that
night!

JACQUES HURY: What hand?

VIOLAINE: That silent hand that clasped mine, and
led me, when I was coming back with my food.

JACQUES HURY: Led you where?

VIOLAINE: Where Pierre de Craon found me.
Under a great mound of sand, a whole cart-load
heaped upon me. Did I place myself there,
all alone?

JACQUES HURY (*rising*): Who has done that?
God's Blood! who has done that?

VIOLAINE: I don't know. It matters little. Do
not curse.

JACQUES HURY: I shall find out the truth about
that.

VIOLAINE: No, you shall find out the truth about nothing.

JACQUES HURY: Tell me all!

VIOLAINE: I have told you all. What would you learn of a blind woman?

JACQUES HURY: You shall not put me off the track.

VIOLAINE: Do not waste words. I have only a little more time to be with you.

JACQUES HURY: I shall always have Mara.

VIOLAINE: She is your wife, and she is my sister, born of the same father and the same mother, and of the same flesh,
Both of us, here beside Monsanvierge.

> (*Silence.*

> (JACQUES *stands a moment motionless, as if trying to control himself. Then he sits down again.*

JACQUES HURY: There are no more recluses at Monsanvierge.

VIOLAINE: What do you say?

JACQUES HURY: The last one died last Christmas. No mouth comes any more to the wicket of the nourishing church of this holy monastery, so the priest tells us who used to give them communion.

VIOLAINE: The mountain of God
Is dead, and we share the heritage, Mara and I.

JACQUES HURY: And Violaine was the secret offshoot
of the Holy Tree, growing from some subter-
ranean root.

God would not have taken her from me, if she
had been entirely filled by me, leaving no part
of her empty,

"God's part," as good women call it.

VIOLAINE: What's to be done? so much the worse!

JACQUES HURY: Stay! do not go!

VIOLAINE: I stay, I am not going.

Tell me, Jacques, do you remember that hour at
noon, and that great scorching sun, and that
spot on the flesh under my breast that I showed
to you?

JACQUES HURY: Ah!

VIOLAINE: You remember? did I not tell you
truly that you could never more tear me out
of your soul?

This of myself is in you for ever. I do not wish
you any more to be happy, it is not proper that
you should laugh,

In this time when you are still far away from me.

JACQUES HURY: Ah! Ah! Violaine!

VIOLAINE: Have this from me, my well-beloved!

The communion on the cross, the bitterness like
the bitterness of myrrh,

Of the sick man who sees the shadow upon the
dial, and of the soul that receives its call!

And for you age is already come. But how hard
it is to renounce when the heart is young!

JACQUES HURY: And from me you have not wanted
to accept anything!

VIOLAINE: Think you that I know nothing about
you, Jacques?

JACQUES HURY: My mother knew me.

VIOLAINE: To me also, O Jacques, you have caused
much pain!

JACQUES HURY: You are a virgin and I have no
part in you.

VIOLAINE: What! must I tell you everything?

JACQUES HURY: What do you still conceal?

VIOLAINE: It is necessary. This is not the time to
keep anything back.

JACQUES HURY: Speak louder.

VIOLAINE: Have they not told you, then, that
your child was dead?

Last year, while you were at Rheims?

JACQUES HURY: Several people told me. But
Mara swears that it only slept.

And I have never been able to draw from her
the whole story.

They say she went to find you.

I should have known everything in time. I
wanted to learn the whole truth.

VIOLAINE: That is true. You have the right to
know all.

JACQUES HURY: What did she go to ask of you?

VIOLAINE: Have you never noticed that the eyes of your little girl are changed?

JACQUES HURY: They are blue now, like yours.

VIOLAINE: It was Christmas night. Yes, Jacques, it is true, she was dead. Her little body was stiff and icy.

I know it; all night I held her in my arms.

JACQUES HURY: Who then restored her to life?

VIOLAINE: God only, and with God the faith and the despair of her mother.

JACQUES HURY: But you had nothing to do with it?

VIOLAINE: O Jacques, to you only I will tell a great mystery.

It is true, when I felt this dead body upon my own, the child of your flesh, Jacques. . . .

JACQUES HURY: Ah, my little Aubaine!

VIOLAINE: You love her very much?

JACQUES HURY: Go on.

VIOLAINE: . . . My heart contracted, and the iron entered into me.

Behold what I held in my arms for my Christmas night, and all that remained of our race, a dead child!

All of yours that I should ever possess in this life!

And I listened to Mara, who read me the Service for this Holy night: the babe who has been given to us, the gospel of Joy.

Ah, do not say that I know nothing of you!
Do not say that I do not know what it is to suffer
for you!
Nor that I do not know the effort and the par-
tition of the woman who gives life!

JACQUES HURY: You do not mean that the child
was really brought back to life?

VIOLAINE: What I know is that it was dead, and
that all of a sudden I felt its head move!
And life burst from me in a flash, at one bound,
and my mortified flesh bloomed again!
Ah, I know what it is, that little blind mouth
that seeks, and those pitiless teeth!

JACQUES HURY: O Violaine!

(*Silence. He makes as if to rise.* VIOLAINE
feebly forces him to remain seated.

VIOLAINE: Do you forgive me now?

JACQUES HURY: Oh, the duplicity of women!
Ah, you are the daughter of your mother!
Tell me! it is not you that you would have me
forgive!

VIOLAINE: Whom, then?

JACQUES HURY: What hand was that which took
yours the other night, and so kindly led you?

VIOLAINE: I do not know.

JACQUES HURY: But I think that I know.

VIOLAINE: You do not know.
Leave that to us, it is an affair between women.

JACQUES HURY: My affair is to have justice done.

VIOLAINE: Ah, leave thy Justice alone!

JACQUES HURY: I know what remains for me to do.

VIOLAINE: You know nothing at all, poor fellow. You have no understanding of women,

And what poor creatures they are, stupid and hard-headed and knowing only one thing.

Do not confuse everything between you and her, as with you and me.

Was it really her hand alone? I do not know. And you do not know either. And of what good would it be to know?

Keep what you have. Forgive.

And you, have you never needed to be forgiven?

JACQUES HURY: I am alone.

VIOLAINE: Not alone, with this beautiful little child I have given back to you,

And Mara, my sister, your wife, of the same flesh as myself. Who, with me, knows you better?

It is necessary for you to have the strength and the deed, it is necessary for you to have a duty plainly laid down and final.

That is why I have this sand in my hair.

JACQUES HURY: Happiness is ended for me.

VIOLAINE: It is ended, what does that matter? Happiness was never promised to you. Work, that is all that is asked of you. (And Monsanvierge belongs only to you now.)

Question the old earth and she will always answer
you with bread and wine.

As for me I have finished with her, and I go
beyond.

Tell me, what is the day you will pass far from
me? It will soon pass.

And when your turn shall come, and when you
see the great door creak and move,

I shall be on the other side and you will find me
waiting. *(Silence.*

JACQUES HURY: O my betrothed, through the
blossoming branches, hail!

VIOLAINE: You remember?

Jacques! Good morning, Jacques!

(The first rays of dawn appear.

And now I must be carried away from here.

JACQUES HURY: Carried away?

VIOLAINE: This is not the place for a leper to die in.

Let me be carried to that shelter my father
built for the poor at the door of Monsanvierge,

*(He makes as if to take her. She waves him
away with her hand.*

No, Jacques, no, not you.

JACQUES HURY: What, not even this last duty
to you?

VIOLAINE: No it is not right that you should touch
me.

Call Pierre de Craon.

He has been a leper, though God has cured him.
He has no horror of me.

And I know that to him I am like a brother,
and woman has no more power over his soul.

> (JACQUES HURY *goes out and returns several
> minutes later with* PIERRE DE CRAON.
> *She does not speak. The two men look at
> her in silence.*

VIOLAINE: Jacques!

JACQUES HURY: Violaine!

VIOLAINE: Has the year been good and the grain
fine and abundant?

JACQUES HURY: So abundant that we do not know
where to put it all.

VIOLAINE: Ah!

How beautiful a great harvest is!

Yes, even now I remember it, and I think it
beautiful.

JACQUES HURY: Yes, Violaine.

VIOLAINE: How beautiful it is

To live! (*speaking low and with deep fervour*) and
how great is the glory of God!

JACQUES HURY: Live, then, and stay with us.

VIOLAINE: But how good it is to die too! When all
is really ended, and over us spreads little by
little

The darkness, as of a deep shade.   (*Silence.*

PIERRE DE CRAON: She does not speak any more.

JACQUES HURY: Take her. Carry her where I
have told you.
For, as to me, she does not wish me to touch her,
Very gently! Gently, gently, I tell you. Do
not hurt her.

> (*They go out*, PIERRE *carrying the body.*
> *The door stands open. Long pause.*

Act Four: Scene Four

On the threshold of the door appears ANNE VERCORS *in the habit of a traveller, a staff in his hand and a sack slung on his back.*

ANNE VERCORS: Open?

Is the house empty, that all the doors should be open?

Who has come in so early before me? or who is it that has gone out?

(He looks around a long time.

I recognize the old room, nothing is changed.

Here is the fireplace, here is the table.

Here is the ceiling with its strong beams.

I am like an animal that smells all around him, and who knows his resting-place and his home.

Hail, house! It is I. Here is the master come back.

Hail, Monsanvierge, lofty dwelling!

From far away, since yesterday morning and the day before, on the top of the hill I recognized the Arch with the five towers.

But why is it that the bells ring no more? neither yesterday nor this morning.

Have I heard in the sky, with the Angel ninefold sonorous, tidings of Jesus brought three times, three times to the heart of Mary.

Monsanvierge! how often I have thought of thy
walls,

While, under my captive feet, I made the water
rise into the garden of the old man of Damascus.
(Oh, the morning, and the implacable afternoon!
Oh, the eternal noria and the eyes we lift
toward Lebanon!)

And all the aromatic odours of exile are little
to me

Compared with this walnut-leaf I crush between
my fingers.

Hail, Earth, powerful and subdued! Here it
is not sand that we plough, and soft alluvium,

But the deep earth itself that we work with the
whole strength of our body and of the six oxen
who pull and form slowly under the plough-
share of the great trench,

And, as far as my eyes can see, everything has
responded to the upheaval man has caused.

Already I have seen all my fields, and perceived
that everything is well cared for. God be
praised! Jacques does his work well.

(*He lays his sack on the table.*

Earth, I have been to seek for thee a little earth,

A little earth for my burial, that which God himself chose for his own at Jerusalem.   (*Pause.*

I would not come back last night. I waited for
daylight.

And I passed the night under a stack of new
straw, thinking, sleeping, praying, looking
around, remembering, giving thanks,
Listening to hear, if I could, the voice of my
wife, or of my daughter Violaine, or of a cry-
ing child.
When I awoke I saw that the night was brighter.
And up there, above the dark crest of Monsanvierge, resplendent, from Arabia,
The morning star rose over France, like a herald
rising in the solitude!
And then I came to the house.

Hallo! Is there anybody here?
(*He raps on the table with his staff.* . . .
*Curtain, which remains down a few min-
utes.*

Act Four: Scene Five

The farther end of the garden. Afternoon of the same day. End of the summer.

The trees are heavy with fruit. The branches of some of them, bending to the ground, are held up by props. The dried and tarnished leaves, mingled with the red and yellow of apples, seem like tapestry.

Below, flooded with light, lies the immense plain as it would be after the harvest; with stubble, and already some ploughed earth. The white roads and the villages can be seen. There are rows of haystacks, looking very small, and here and there a poplar. Far away, in another direction, are flocks of sheep. The shadows of large clouds pass over the plain.

In the middle, where the scene descends toward the background, from which the tops of the trees in a little wood are seen to emerge, there is a semicircular stone bench, reached by three steps, and with lions' heads at each end of its back. ANNE VERCORS *is sitting there, with* JACQUES HURY *at his right side.*

ANNE VERCORS: The golden end of Autumn
Will soon
Despoil the fruit tree and the vine.
And in the morning the white sun,

A single flash of a fireless diamond, will blend
    with the white vesture of the earth:
And the evening is near when he who walks
    beneath the aspen
Shall hear the last leaf on its summit.
Now, behold, making equal the days and nights,
Counterpoising the long hours of labour with its
    projecting sign, athwart the celestial Door
Interposes the royal Balance.

JACQUES HURY: Father, since thou hast been gone,
    Everything, the painful story, and the plot of
    these women, and the pitfall made to take
    us in,
    Thou know'st, and I have told thee
    Still another thing, with my mouth against thine
    ear,
    Where is thy wife? where is thy daughter Violaine?
    And lo, thou talkest of the straw we twist, and
    of the great black grape
    Which fills the hand of the vine-dresser, the
    hand he thrusts under the vine-branch!
    Already
    The crooked Scorpion and the retreating Sagit-
    tarius
    Have appeared on the dial of night.

ANNE VERCORS: Let the old man exult in the warm
    season! O truly blessed place! O bosom of the
    Fatherland! O grateful, fecund earth!

145

The carts passing along the road
Leave straw among the fruited branches!

JACQUES HURY: O Violaine! O cruel Violaine!
desire of my soul, you have betrayed me!

O hateful garden! O love useless and denied!
O garden planted in an evil hour!

Sweet Violaine! perfidious Violaine! Oh, the
silence and the depth of woman!

Art thou then really gone, my soul?

Having deceived me, she goes away; and having
undeceived me, with fatal sweet words,

She goes again, and I, bearing this poisoned
arrow, it will be necessary

That I live on and on! like the beast we take
by the horn, drawing his head out of the
manger,

Like the horse we loose from the single-tree in
the evening with a lash of the whip on his
back!

O ox, it is thou that walkest ahead, but we two
make but one team.

Only that the furrow be made, that is all they
ask of us.

That is why everything that was not necessary to
my task, everything has been taken away from
me.

ANNE VERCORS: Monsanvierge is dead, and the
fruit of your labour is for you alone.

JACQUES HURY: It is true.   (*Silence.*

ANNE VERCORS: Have they looked well to pro-
visioning the chapel for to-morrow?

Is there enough to eat and drink for all those we
shall have to entertain?

JACQUES HURY: Old man! It is your daughter
we are going to lay in the earth, and behold
what you find to say!

Surely you have never loved her! But the old
man, like the miser who after warming his
hands at his pot of embers hoards their heat in
his bosom,

He suffices for himself alone.

ANNE VERCORS: Everything must be done.

Things must be done honourably.

. . . Elisabeth, my wife, hidden heart!

(*Enter* PIERRE DE CRAON.

ANNE VERCORS: Is everything ready?

PIERRE DE CRAON: They are working at the coffin.

They are digging the grave where you ordered,

Close up by the church there, near that of the
last chaplain, your brother.

Within it they have put the earth you brought
back.

A great black ivy-vine

Comes out of the priestly tomb, and, crossing the
wall,

Enters almost into the sealed arch.

. . . To-morrow, in the early morning. Everything is ready.

> (JACQUES HURY *weeps, his face in his cloak.*
> *In the path is seen a nun, like a woman*
> *who hunts for flowers.*

ANNE VERCORS: What are you looking for, Sister?

VOICE OF THE NUN (*hollow and smothered*): Some
flowers, to lay on her heart, between her
hands.

ANNE VERCORS: There are no more flowers, there
is nothing but fruit.

JACQUES HURY: Push aside the leaves and you
will find the last violet!

And the Immortelle is still in the bud, and nothing is left to us but the dahlia and the poppy.

> (*The nun is no longer there.*

PIERRE DE CRAON: The two Sisters, who care for
the sick, one quite young the other very old,

Have dressed her, and Mara has sent her wedding-
dress for her.

Truly, she was only a leper, but she was honourable in the sight of God.

She reposes in a deep sleep

As one who knows in whose care she is.

I saw her before they had laid her in the coffin.

Her body is still supple.

Oh, while the Sister finished dressing her, with
her arm around her waist,

Holding her in a sitting posture, how her head
    fell backward
Like that of the still warm partridge the hunter
    picks in his hand!

ANNE VERCORS: My child! my little daughter I car-
ried in my arms before she knew how to walk!
The fat little girl who awoke with bursts of
    laughter in her little sabot of a bed.
All that is over. Ah! ah! O God! Alas!

PIERRE DE CRAON: Don't you want to see her
    before they nail down the coffin-lid?

ANNE VERCORS: No. The child disowned
Goes away secretly.

JACQUES HURY: Never again in this life shall I
    see her face.

> (PIERRE DE CRAON *sits down at the left of*
> ANNE VERCORS. *Long pause. The sound
> of a hammer on planks. They remain
> silent, listening.*
>
> MARA *is seen to pass at the side of the stage
> holding a child in her arms wrapped in a
> black shawl. Then she re-enters slowly at
> the back, and comes and stands in front of
> the bench where the three men are sitting.
> They stare at her, except* JACQUES HURY,
> *who looks at the ground.*

MARA (*her head lowered*): Hail, father! Hail to
    you all.

You stare at me and I know what you think:
"Violaine is dead.
The beautiful ripe fruit, the good golden fruit
Has fallen from the branch, and, bitter without,
    hard as a stone within,
Only the wintry nut remains to us." Who loves
    me? Who has ever loved me?
        (*She lifts her head with a savage gesture.*
Well! here I am! what have you to say to me?
Say everything! What have you against me?
What makes you look at me like that, with
    your eyes saying: It is thou! It is true, it
    is I!
It is true, it was I who killed her,
It was I the other night who took her by the
    hand, having gone to seek her,
While Jacques was not there,
And I who made her fall into the sandpit, and
    who turned over upon her
That loaded cart. Everything was ready, there
    was only a bolt to pull out,
I did that,
Jacques! and it is I, too, who said to my mother,
Violaine — to talk to her that day when you came
    back from Braine.
For I longed ardently to marry you, and if I
    could not I had decided to hang myself the
    day of your wedding.

Now God, who sees into hearts, had already let her
take the leprosy.
—But Jacques never stopped thinking of her.
That is why I killed her.
What then? What else was there to do? What
more could be done
So that the one I love and who is mine
Should be mine entirely, as I am his entirely,
And that Violaine should be shut out?
I did what I could.
And you in your turn, answer! Your Violaine
that you loved,
How then did you love her, and which was worth
the most,
Your love, do you think, or my hatred?
You all loved her! and here is her father who
abandons her, and her mother who advises
her!
And her betrothed, how he has believed in her!
Certainly you loved her,
As we say we love a gentle animal, a pretty flower,
and that was all the feeling there was in your
love!
Mine was of another kind;
Blind, never letting go anything once taken, like
a deaf thing that does not hear!
For him to have me entirely, it was necessary to
me to have him entirely!

What have I done after all that I must defend
myself? who has been the most faithful to him,
I or Violaine?

Violaine who betrayed him for I know not what
leper, giving in, said she, to God's council in a
kiss?

I honour God. Let him stay where he is! Our
miserable life is so short! Let him leave us
in peace!

Is it my fault if I loved Jacques? was it for
my happiness, or for the burning away of my
soul?

What could I do to defend myself, I who am not
beautiful, nor agreeable, a poor woman who
can only give pain?

That is why I killed her in my despair!

O poor, unskilful crime!

O disgrace to her that no one loves and with whom
nothing succeeds! What ought to have been
done, since I loved him and he did not love
me? (*She turns toward* JACQUES.

And you, O Jacques, why do you not speak?

Why turn you your face to the ground, without
a word to say,

Like Violaine, the day when you accused her un-
justly?

Do you not know me? I am your wife.

Truly I know that I do not seem to you either

beautiful or agreeable, but look, I have dressed
myself for you, I have added to that pain that
I can give you. And I am the sister of Violaine.

It is born of pain! This love is not born of
joy, it is born of pain! the pain which suffices
for those who have no joy!

No one is glad to see it, ah, it is not the flower
in its season,

But that which is under the flowers that wither,
the earth itself, the miserly earth under the
grass, the earth that never fails!

Know me then!

I am your wife and you can do nothing to change
that!

One inseparable flesh, the contact by the centre
and by the soul, and for confirmation this
mysterious parentage between us two.

Which is, that I have had a child of yours.

I have committed a great crime, I have killed my
sister; but I have not sinned against you. And
I tell you that you have nothing to reproach
me with. And what do the others matter to
me?

That is what I had to say, and now do what you
will.   (*Silence.*

ANNE VERCORS: What she says is true. Go,
Jacques, forgive her!

153

JACQUES HURY: Come then, Mara.

> (*She comes nearer and stands before them,
> forming with her child a single object upon
> which the two men extend together their
> right hands. Their arms cross, and*
> JACQUES' *hand is laid on the head of the
> child, that of* ANNE *on the head of* MARA.

JACQUES HURY: It is Violaine who forgives you.
It is through her, Mara, that I forgive you.
Guilty woman, it is she who reunites us.

MARA: Alas! alas! dead words and without a
ray of light!

O Jacques, I am no longer the same! There is
something in me that is ended. Have no fear.
All that is nothing to me.

Something in me is broken, and I am left without
strength, like a woman widowed and without
children.

> (*The child laughs vaguely and looks all
> around, with little cries of delight.*

ANNE VERCORS (*caressing it*): Poor Violaine! And
you, little child! How blue its eyes are!

MARA (*melting into tears*): Father! father! ah!
It was dead, and it was she who brought it back
to life!

> (*She goes away, and sits down alone.
> The sun goes down. It rains here and there
> on the plain, and the lines of the rain can*

*be seen crossing the rays of the sun. An
immense rainbow unfurls.*

VOICE OF A CHILD: Hi! Hi! look at the beautiful
rainbow!

> (*Other voices cease in the distance. Great
> flocks of pigeons fly about, turning, scatter-
> ing, and alighting here and there in the
> stubble.*

ANNE VERCORS: The earth is set free. The
place is empty.

The harvest is all gathered, and the birds of
heaven

Pick up the lost grain.

PIERRE DE CRAON: Summer is over, the season
sleeps in a time of quiet, everywhere the foliage
rustles in the breeze of September.

The sky has turned blue again, and while the
partridges call from their covert,

The buzzard soars in the liquid air.

JACQUES HURY: Everything is yours. Father! take
back again all this property you vested in me.

ANNE VERCORS: No, Jacques, I no longer possess
anything, and this is no more mine. He who
went away will not return, and that which is
once given cannot be

Taken back. Here is a new Combernon, a new
Monsanvierge.

PIERRE DE CRAON: The other is dead. The virgin

mountain is dead, and the scar in her side will never open again.

ANNE VERCORS: It is dead. My wife, too, is dead, my daughter is dead, the holy Maid

Has been burned and thrown to the winds, not one of her bones remains on the earth.

But the King and the Pope have been given back again to France and to the whole world.

The schism comes to an end, and once more the Throne rises above all men.

I returned by Rome, I kissed the foot of Saint Peter, I ate the consecrated bread standing with people from the Four Divisions of the Earth,

While the bells of the Quirinal and of the Lateran, and the voice of Santa Maria Maggiore,

Saluted the ambassadors of these new nations who come from the Orient and the Occident all together into the City,

Asia found again, and this Atlantic world beyond the Pillars of Hercules!

And this very evening when the Angelus shall ring, at the same hour when the star Al-Zohar glows in the unfurled heaven,

Begins the year of Jubilee which the new Pope grants,

The annulment of debts, the liberation of prisoners, the suspension of war, the closing of the courts, the restitution of all property.

PIERRE DE CRAON: Truce for one year and peace for one day only.

ANNE VERCORS: What does it matter? peace is good, but war will find us armed.

O Pierre! this is a time when women and new-born infants teach sages and old men!

Here am I shocked like a Jew because the face of the Church is darkened, and because she totters on her road forsaken by all men.

And I wanted once more to clasp the empty tomb, to put my hand in the hole left by the cross.

But my little daughter Violaine has been wiser.

Is the object of life only to live? will the feet of God's children be fastened to this wretched earth?

It is not to live, but to die, and not to hew the cross, but to mount upon it, and to give all that we have, laughing!

There is joy, there is freedom, there is grace, there is eternal youth! and as God lives, the blood of the old man on the sacrificial cloth, near that of the young man,

Makes a stain as red and fresh as that of the yearling lamb!

O Violaine! child of grace! flesh of my flesh! As far as the smoky fire of my farm is distant from the morning star,

When on the sun's breast that beautiful virgin
lays her illumined head,

May thy father see thee on high through all eternity in the place which has been kept for thee!

As God lives, where the little child goes the
father should go also!

What is the worth of the world compared to life?
and what is the worth of life if not to be given?

And why torment ourselves when it is so simple
to obey?

It is thus that Violaine follows at once without
hesitation the hand that takes hers.

PIERRE DE CRAON: O father! I was the last who
held her in my arms, because she entrusted
herself to Pierre de Craon, knowing that there
is no longer in his heart the desire of the flesh.

And the young body of this divine brother lay
in my arms like a tree that has been cut down
and droops

Already, as the glowing colour of the pomegranate
blossoms everywhere flames from the bud that
can no longer sheathe it,

So the splendour of the angel that knows not
death embraces our little sister.

The odour of Paradise exhaled in my arms from
this broken tabernacle.

Do not weep, Jacques, my friend.

ANNE VERCORS: Do not weep, my son.

JACQUES HURY: Pierre, give me back that ring she
gave thee.

PIERRE DE CRAON: I cannot!

Any more than the ripened spike of corn can
give back the seed in the earth from which
sprang its stem.

Of that bit of gold I have made a fiery gem.

And the vessel of everlasting Day where the seed
of the ultimate goodness of saintly souls is
treasured.

Justitia is finished and lacks only the woman
that I shall set there at the blossoming of my
supreme lily.

ANNE VERCORS: You are powerful in works, Pierre,
and I have seen on my way the churches you
have brought to birth.

PIERRE DE CRAON: Blessed be God who has made
me a father of churches,

And who has endowed my soul with understanding and the sense of the three dimensions!

And who has debarred me as a leper and freed
me from all temporal care,

To the end that I should raise up from the soil
of France Ten Wise Virgins whose oil is never
exhausted, and who compose a vessel of prayers!

What is this *soul*, or bolt of wood, that the lute-
maker inserts between the front and the back
of his instrument,

Compared to this great enclosed lyre, and of
these columnar Powers in the night, whose
number and distance I have calculated?

Never from the outside do I carve an image.

But, like father Noah, from the middle of my
enormous Arch,

I work from within, and see everything rise
simultaneously around me!

And what is matter which the hand can chisel
compared to the spirit we strive to enshrine,

Or to the hallowed space left empty by a rever-
ent soul shrinking back in the presence of its
God?

Nothing is too deep for me: my wells descend
as far as the waters of the Mother-spring.

Nothing is too high for the spire that mounts to
heaven and steals God's lightning from him!

Pierre de Craon will die, but the Ten Virgins,
his daughters,

Will remain like the Widow's cruse

In which the flower and the sacred measures of
the oil and wine are renewed for ever.

ANNE VERCORS: Yes, Pierre. Whoever trusts himself to stone will not be deceived.

PIERRE DE CRAON: Oh, how beautiful is stone,
and how soft it is in the hands of the architect!
and how right and beautiful a thing is his whole
completed work!

How faithful is stone, and how well it preserves
the idea, and what shadows it makes!
And if a vine grows well on the least bit of wall,
and the rosebush above it blooms,
How beautiful it is, and how true it is altogether!
Have you seen my little church of l'Epine, which
is like a glowing brasier and a rosebush in full
bloom?
And Saint Jean de Vertus like a handsome young
man in the midst of the Craie Champenoise?
And Mont-Saint Martin which will be mellow
in fifty years?
And Saint-Thomas of Fond-d'Ardenne that you
can hear in the evening bellowing like a bull
in the midst of its marshes?
But Justitia that I have made last, Justitia my
daughter is more beautiful!

ANNE VERCORS: I shall go there and leave my
staff for a thank-offering.

PIERRE DE CRAON: She is dedicated in my heart,
nothing is lacking, she is whole.
And for the roof,
I have found the stone I sought, not quarried by
iron,
Softer than alabaster and closer-grained than a
grindstone.
As the fragile teeth of the little Justitia serve as
a foundation for my great structure,

161

So also at the summit, in the wide sky, I shall
set this other Justice

Violaine the leper in glory, Violaine the blind in
the sight of everybody.

And I shall make her with her hands crossed on
her breast, like the spike of grain still half-
prisoned in its tegmen,

And her eyes blindfolded.

ANNE VERCORS: Why blindfolded?

PIERRE DE CRAON: That, seeing not, she may the
better hear

The sounds of the city and the fields, and man's
voice at the same time with the voice of God.

For she is Justice herself, who listens and con-
ceives in her heart the perfect harmony.

This is she who is a refuge from storms, and a
shade from the heat at the rising of the dog-
star.

JACQUES HURY: But Violaine is not a stone for me,
and stone does not suffice me!

And I do not wish the light of her beautiful eyes
to be veiled!

ANNE VERCORS: The light of her soul is with us.
I have not lost thee, Violaine! How beautiful
thou art, my child!

And how beautiful is the bride when on her wed-
ding-day she shows herself to her father in her
splendid wedding-gown, sweetly embarrassed.

Walk before me, Violaine, my child, and I will
follow thee. But sometimes turn thy face
toward me, that I may see thine eyes!

Violaine! Elisabeth! soon again I shall be with
you.

As for you, Jacques, perform your task in your
turn, as I have done mine! The end is near.

It is here, the end of all that is given me of the
day, of the year, and of my own life!

It is six o'clock. The shadow of the Grès-qui-
va-boire reaches the brook.

Winter comes, night comes; yet a little more night,
A short watch!

All my life I have worked with the Sun and aided
him in his task.

But now, by the fireside, in the light of the lamp,
All alone I must begin the night.

PIERRE DE CRAON: O husbandman, your work is
finished. See the empty land, see the harvested earth, and already the plough attacks
the stubble!

And now, what you have begun it is my part to
complete.

As you have opened the furrow, I dig the pit
wherein to preserve the grain, I prepare the
tabernacle.

And as it is not you who cause the harvest to
ripen, but the sun, so is it also with grace.

And nothing, unless it issue from the seed, can
develop into the ear.

And certainly, Justice is beautiful. But how
much more beautiful

Is this fruitful tree of mankind, which the seed
of the Eucharist engenders and makes grow.

This too makes one complete whole, unified.

Ah, if all men understood architecture as I do,

Who would willingly fail to follow his vocation
and renounce the sacred place assigned to him
in the Temple?

ANNE VERCORS: Pierre de Craon, you have many
thoughts, but for me this setting sun suffices.

All my life I have done the same thing that he
does, cultivating the earth, rising and returning
home with him.

And now I go into the night, and I am not afraid,
and I know that there too all is clear and in
order, in the season of this great heavenly
winter which sets all things in motion.

The night sky where everything is at work, and
which is like a great ploughing, and a room
with only one person in it.

And there the eternal Ploughman drives the seven
oxen, with his gaze set upon a fixed star,

As ours is set upon the green branch that marks
the end of the furrow.

The sun and I, side by side

Have worked, and the product of our work does not concern us.   Mine is done.

I bow to what must be, and now I am willing to be dissolved.

And herein lies peace for him who knows it, and joy and grief in equal parts.

My wife is dead.   Violaine is dead.   That is right.

I do not desire to hold any more that weak and wrinkled old hand.   And as for Violaine, when she was eight years old, when she came and threw herself against my legs,

How I loved that strong little body!   And little by little the impetuous, frolicsome roughness of the laughing child

Melted into the tenderness of the maiden, into the pain and heaviness of love, and when I went away

I saw already in her eyes one unknown blossom among the flowers of her springtime.

PIERRE DE CRAON: The call of death, like a solemn lily.

ANNE VERCORS: Blessed be death in which all the petitions in the Paternoster are satisfied.

PIERRE DE CRAON: For my part, it was by herself and from her innocent lips

That I received freedom and dismissal from this life.

> (*The sun is in the western sky, as high as a tall tree.*

ANNE VERCORS: Behold the sun in the sky,
As he is in the pictures where the Master awakes
the workman at the Eleventh Hour.

> (*The door of the barn is heard to creak.*

JACQUES HURY: What is that?

ANNE VERCORS: They have come to the barn for
straw
To lay in the bottom of the grave.

> (*Silence: — Sound in the distance of a washer-*
> *woman beating linen.*

VOICE OF A CHILD (*without*):
Marguerite of Paris, pray!
Lend to me thy shoes of gray!
To walk in Paradise a way!
How fair it is!
How warm it is!
I hear the little bird say it is!
He goes pa — a — a — a!

JACQUES HURY: That is not the door of the barn,
it is the sound of the tomb opening!

And, having looked at me with her blind eyes,
she that I loved passes to the other side.

And I too, I have looked at her like one who is
blind, and I did not doubt without proofs.

I never doubted her who accused her.

I have made my choice, and she that I chose has
been given to me. What shall I say? It is
right.

It is right.

Happiness is not for me, but desire! it will never be torn from me.

And not Violaine, radiant and unblemished,

But the leper bending over me with a bitter smile and the devouring wound in her side!

(*Silence.*

(*The sun is behind the trees. It shines through the branches. The shadows of the leaves cover the ground and the seated people. Here and there a golden bee shines in the sunny interstices.*

ANNE VERCORS: Here am I seated, and from the top of the mountain I see all the country at my feet.

And I recognize the roads, and I count the farms and villages, and I know them by name, and all the people who live in them.

The plain is lost to view toward the north.

And elsewhere, rising again, the hill surrounds this village like a theatre.

And everywhere, all the while,

Green and pink in the spring, blue and flaxen in the summer, brown in winter or all white with snow,

Before me, at my side, around me,

I see always the Earth, like an unchanging sky all painted with changing colours.

Having a form as much its own as a person's, it
is always there present with me.

Now that is finished.

How many times have I risen from my bed and
gone to my work!

And now here is evening, and the sun brings
home the men and the animals as if he led
them by his hand.

> (*He raises himself slowly and painfully, and
> slowly stretches out his arms to their full
> length, while the sun, grown yellow, covers
> him.*

Ah! ah!

Here am I stretching out my arms in the rays
of the sun.

Evening is come! Have pity upon every man,
Lord, in that hour when he has finished his
task and stands before Thee like a child whose
hands are being examined.

Mine are free. My day is finished. I have
planted the grain and I have harvested it, and
with this bread that I have made all my children have made their communion.

Now I have finished.

A moment ago there was some one with me.

And now, wife and child having gone away,

I remain alone to say grace at the empty table.

Both of them are dead, but I,

I live, on the threshold of death, and I am filled with inexplicable joy!

> (*The Angelus is rung from the church down below. First toll of three strokes.*

JACQUES HURY (*hollowly*): The Angel of God proclaims peace to us, and the child thrills in the bosom of its mother.   (*Second toll.*

PIERRE DE CRAON: "Men of little faith, why do you weep?"   (*Third toll.*

ANNE VERCORS: "Because I go to my father and to your father."

> (*Profound silence. Then peal.*

PIERRE DE CRAON: Thus the Angelus speaks as if with three voices, in May

When the unmarried man comes home, having buried his mother,

"Voice-of-the-Rose" speaks in the silvery evening.

O Violaine! O woman through whom comes temptation!

For, not yet knowing what I would do, I turned my eyes where you then did turn thine.

Truly I have always thought that joy was a good thing.

But now I have everything!

I possess everything, under my hands, and I am like a person who, seeing a tree laden with fruit,

And having mounted a ladder, feels the thick branches yield under his body.

I must talk under the tree, like a flute which is
neither low nor shrill! How the water
Raises me! Thanksgiving unseals the stone of
my heart!
How I live, thus! How I grow greater, thus
mingled with my God, like the vine and the
olive-tree.

> (*The sun goes down.* MARA *turns her head
> toward her husband and looks at him.*

JACQUES HURY: See her, looking at me. See her
returning to me with the night!

> (*Sound of a cracked bell near by. First toll.*

ANNE VERCORS: It is the little bell of the sisters
that rings the Angelus in its turn.

> (*Silence. Then another bell is heard, very
> high up, at Monsanvierge, sounding in its
> turn the triple toll, admirably sonorous and
> solemn.*

JACQUES HURY: Listen!

PIERRE DE CRAON: A miracle!

ANNE VERCORS: It is Monsanvierge come to life again!
The Angelus, ringing once more, brings to the listening heavens and earth the wonted tidings.

PIERRE DE CRAON: Yes, Voice-of-the-Rose, God
is born!

> (*Second toll of the bell of the sisters.
> It strikes the third note just as Monsan-
> vierge strikes the first.*

ANNE VERCORS: God makes himself man.

JACQUES HURY: He is dead!

PIERRE DE CRAON: He is risen!

> (*Third toll of the bell of the sisters. Then the peal.*
>
> *Pause. Then, nearly lost in the distance, are heard the three strokes of the third toll up on the heights.*

ANNE VERCORS: This is not the toll of the Angelus, it is the communion bells!

PIERRE DE CRAON: The three strokes are gathered like an ineffable sacrifice into the bosom of the Virgin without sin.

> (*Their faces are turned toward the heights, they listen as if awaiting the peal, which does not come.*

EXPLICIT.